TEACHER'S PET PUBLICATIONS

LITPLAN TEACHER PACK
for
Gulliver's Travels
based on the book by
Jonathan Swift

Written by
Mary B. Collins & Barbara M. Linde

© 1995 Teacher's Pet Publications
All Rights Reserved

This **LitPlan** for Jonathan Swift's
Gulliver's Travels
has been brought to you by Teacher's Pet Publications, Inc.

Copyright Teacher's Pet Publications 1995
11504 Hammock Point
Berlin MD 21811

Only the student materials in this unit plan (such as worksheets, study questions, and tests) may be reproduced multiple times for use in the purchaser's classroom.

For any additional copyright questions,
contact Teacher's Pet Publications.

www.tpet.com

TABLE OF CONTENTS - *Gulliver's Travels*

Introduction	4
Unit Objectives	6
Reading Assignment Sheet	7
Unit Outline	8
Study Questions (Short Answer)	11
Quiz/Study Questions (Multiple Choice)	27
Pre-Reading Vocabulary Worksheets	53
Lesson One (Introductory Lesson)	75
Nonfiction Assignment Sheet	84
Oral Reading Evaluation Form	85
Writing Assignment 1	79
Writing Assignment 2	89
Writing Assignment 3	97
Writing Evaluation Form	90
Vocabulary Review Activities	100
Extra Writing Assignments/Discussion ?s	80
Unit Review Activities	99
Unit Tests	107
Unit Resource Materials	143
Vocabulary Resource Materials	159

INTRODUCTION

This unit has been designed to develop students' reading, writing, thinking, listening and speaking skills through exercises and activities related to *Gulliver's Travels* by Jonathan Swift. It includes twenty-one lessons, supported by extra resource materials.

The **introductory lesson** introduces students to one main theme of the novel (man's worst vice is pride) through a bulletin board activity. Following the introductory activity, students are given an explanation of how the activity relates to the book they are about to read.

The **reading assignments** are approximately thirty pages each; some are a little shorter while others are a little longer. Students have approximately 15 minutes of pre-reading work to do prior to each reading assignment. This pre-reading work involves reviewing the study questions for the assignment and doing some vocabulary work for 8 to 10 vocabulary words they will encounter in their reading.

The **study guide questions** are fact-based questions; students can find the answers to these questions right in the text. These questions come in two formats: short answer or multiple choice. The best use of these materials is probably to use the short answer version of the questions as study guides for students (since answers will be more complete), and to use the multiple choice version for occasional quizzes. If your school has the appropriate machinery, it might be a good idea to make transparencies of your answer keys for the overhead projector.

The **vocabulary work** is intended to enrich students' vocabularies as well as to aid in the students' understanding of the book. Prior to each reading assignment, students will complete a two-part worksheet for approximately 8 to 10 vocabulary words in the upcoming reading assignment. Part I focuses on students' use of general knowledge and contextual clues by giving the sentence in which the word appears in the text. Students are then to write down what they think the words mean based on the words' usage. Part II gives students dictionary definitions of the words and has them match the words to the correct definitions based on the words' contextual usage. Students should then have an understanding of the words when they meet them in the text.

After each reading assignment, students will go back and formulate answers for the study guide questions. Discussion of these questions serves as a **review** of the most important events and ideas presented in the reading assignments.

After students complete extra discussion questions, there is a **vocabulary review** lesson which pulls together all of the separate vocabulary lists for the reading assignments and gives students a review of all of the words they have studied.

Following the reading of the book, two lessons are devoted to the **extra discussion questions/writing assignments**. These questions focus on interpretation, critical analysis and personal response, employing a variety of thinking skills and adding to the students' understanding of the novel. These questions are done as a **group activity**. Using the information they have acquired so far through individual work and class discussions, students get together to further examine the text and to brainstorm ideas relating to the themes of the novel.

The group activity is followed by a **reports and discussion** session in which the groups share their ideas about the book with the entire class; thus, the entire class gets exposed to many different ideas regarding the themes and events of the book.

There are three **writing assignments** in this unit, each with the purpose of informing, persuading, or having students express personal opinions. The first assignment asks the students to interpret events from the novel and express their personal opinion. The second assignment is to inform: students will create a travelogue based on a personal journey. The third assignment is to persuade: students will write to Lemuel Gulliver and persuade him to rejoin the company of his family and countrymen.

In addition, there is a **nonfiction reading assignment**. Students are required to read a piece of nonfiction related in some way to *Gulliver's Travels*. After reading their nonfiction pieces, students will fill out a worksheet on which they answer questions regarding facts, interpretation, criticism, and personal opinions. During one class period, students make **oral presentations** about the nonfiction pieces they have read. This not only exposes all students to a wealth of information, it also gives students the opportunity to practice **public speaking**.

The **review lesson** pulls together all of the aspects of the unit. The teacher is given four or five choices of activities or games to use which all serve the same basic function of reviewing all of the information presented in the unit.

The **unit test** comes in two formats: all multiple choice-matching-true/false or with a mixture of matching, short answer, and composition. As a convenience, two different tests for each format have been included.

There are additional **support materials** included with this unit. The **extra activities packet** includes suggestions for an in-class library, crossword and word search puzzles related to the novel, and extra vocabulary worksheets. There is a list of **bulletin board ideas** which gives the teacher suggestions for bulletin boards to go along with this unit. In addition, there is a list of **extra class activities** the teacher could choose from to enhance the unit or as a substitution for an exercise the teacher might feel is inappropriate for his/her class. **Answer keys** are located directly after the **reproducible student materials** throughout the unit. The student materials may be reproduced for use in the teacher's classroom without infringement of copyrights. No other portion of this unit may be reproduced without the written consent of Teacher's Pet Publications, Inc.

UNIT OBJECTIVES *Gulliver's Travels*

1. Through reading *Gulliver's Travels* students will study Swift's perception of the nature of man.

2. Students will study Swift's writing techniques to better understand the value of satire, irony and other devices he uses.

3. Students will compare and contrast characters to gain a better understanding of Swifts' portraits of human nature.

4. Students will practice reading aloud and silently to improve their skills in each area.

5. Students will answer questions to demonstrate their knowledge and understanding of the main events and characters in Gulliver's Travels as they relate to the author's theme and character development.

6. Students will practice writing through a variety of writing assignments.

   7. The writing assignments in this are geared to several purposes:
      a. To check the students' reading comprehension
      b. To make students think about the ideas presented by the novel
      c. To make students put those ideas into perspective
      d. To encourage critical and logical thinking
      e. To provide the opportunity to practice good grammar and
         improve students' use of the English language.

7. Students will read aloud, report, and participate in large and small group discussions to improve their public speaking and personal interaction skills.

READING ASSIGNMENT SHEET *Gulliver's Travels*

Date to be Assigned	Chapters	Completion Date (Prior to Class on This Date)
	One I-IV	
	One V-VIII	
	Two I-IV	
	Two V-VIII	
	Three I-V	
	Three VI-XI	
	Four I-V	
	Four VI-IX	
	Four X-XII	

UNIT OUTLINE - *Gulliver's Travels*

1 Unit Introduction Writing Assignment 1	2 Nonfiction Assignment PVR One I-IV	3 Study ?s One I-IV	4 PVR One V-VIII Study ?s One V-VIII
5 PVR Two I-IV Study ?? Two I-IV	6 PVR Two V-VIII Study ?s Two V-VIII	7 Writing Assignment 2	8 PVR Three I-V Study ?? Three I-V
9 PVR Three VI-XI Study ?s Three VI-XI	10 PVR Four I-V Study ?? Four I-V	11 PVR Four VI-IX Study ?? Four VI-IX	12 PVR Four X-XII Study ?? Four X-XII
13 Writing Assignment 1	14 Group Activity	15 Group Activity	16 Reports & Discussion
17 Nonfiction Discussion	18 Writing Assignment 3	19 Review	20 Vocabulary Review
21 Extra Review	22 Test		

Key: P = Preview Study Questions   V = Vocabulary Work   R = Read

STUDY QUESTIONS

SHORT ANSWER STUDY GUIDE QUESTIONS - *Gulliver's Travels*

Book One - I-IV
1. Who is the narrator, and what does he do for work?
2. How did Gulliver get to Lilliput?
3. Briefly describe the Lilliputians physical appearance.
4. What physical characteristic differentiates the Emperor of Lilliput from his subjects?
5. What kind of living accommodations did the Emperor provide for Gulliver?
6. The Emperor delivered six Lilliputians who had "attacked" Gulliver to him for justice. What did Gulliver do with them?
7. When the Lilliputians try to decide what to do with Gulliver what two means of death do they consider before deciding to let him live?
8. For what purpose do the Lilliputians learn rope dancing and "leaping and creeping"?
9. Identify Skyresh Bolgolam.
10. What were Gulliver's nine conditions of freedom?
11. What are the two political factions in Lilliput?
12. About what are the Lilliputians and Blefuscuians fighting?

Book One - V - VIII
1. How did Gulliver help Lilliput against the Blefuscuians?
2. The Emperor wanted Gulliver to do more to help him finally crush the Blefuscuians so he could be emperor of all the lands. What was Gulliver's response?
3. Briefly describe the Lilliputian educational system.
4. Identify Flimnap.
5. What crime did the Lilliputians consider to be greater than theft?
6. How were citizens who obeyed the laws rewarded?
7. What were the Articles of Impeachment against Gulliver?
8. What means of death for Gulliver did the Treasurer and Admiral offer as suggestions?
9. How did the Council decide to punish Gulliver for his crimes?
10. How did Gulliver escape?
11. Why did Gulliver leave Blefuscu?
12. How did Gulliver leave Blefuscu and return to England?
13. In what ways did Gulliver profit financially from his adventure to Lilliput?

Book Two I - IV
1. How did Gulliver get to Brobdingnag?
2. Give a brief physical description of the residents of Brobdingnag.
3. Who found Gulliver and where did they take him?
4. What "accidents" happened to Gulliver in his first afternoon in the farmer's house?
5. Who or what were Grildrig, Glumdalclitch and Splacknuck?
6. Why did the farmer take Gulliver to market places?
7. How did Gulliver meet the Queen?
8. How did Gulliver and Glumdalclitch end up living with the King and Queen?
9. Where did Gulliver say the kingdom of Brobdingnag was located?
10. What was the Kings' reaction to Gulliver's accounts of English manners, religion, laws and government?
11. Why was the Queen's dwarf mean to Gulliver?
12. How was Gulliver transported during his stay in Brobdingnag?

Book Two - V - VIII
1. What "ridiculous and troublesome accidents" happened to Gulliver?
2. Why did Gulliver ask Glumdalclitch not to take him to the Maids of Honor anymore?
3. What did the monkey do to Gulliver?
4. Why did Gulliver attempt to jump over the cow dung, and what happened?
5. How did Gulliver attempt to please the King and Queen - and why did he do it?
6. After Gulliver took great pride in telling the King about England over the period of about a week, what was the King's reaction?
7. What gift did Gulliver wish to give to the King (so the King would have a more favorable impression of him)? What was the King's reaction?
8. What was Gulliver's opinion of the learning of the people of Brobdingnag?
9. How long did Gulliver stay in Brobdingnag?
10. How did Gulliver leave Brobdingnag, and get back to England?
11. What was the Captain's, and then Gulliver's wife's reaction to his behavior when they first encountered him after his journey?

Book Three - I - V
1. How did Gulliver get to Laputa?
2. On what bizarre object did Gulliver find people?
3. Briefly describe the people Gulliver saw.
4. Identify the use of a flapper.
5. In what way was Gulliver's first meal in Laputa odd?
6. Why didn't Gulliver's new, tailor-made clothes fit?
7. How did Gulliver describe the Laputians?
8. Describe the lifestyle of the women who lived on the island.

9. The King has two methods of keeping his towns obedient. What are they?
10. Identify Munodi.
11. How and why were Munodi's lands and home different from others in the area?
12. What was the purpose of the Academy of Projectors?
13. What's the problem with the Academy?
14. What were some of the projects Gulliver saw Professors attempting at the Academy?
15. What common characteristics did these projects have?
16. How were the professors trying to improve the language of the country?

Book Three VI - XI
1. What did Gulliver think of the things the political projectors were proposing, and why?
2. Why did Gulliver want to go to Luggnagg?
3. Why did Gulliver go to Glubbdubdrib?
4. What unusual power does the Governor of Glubbdubdrib have?
5. Who were some of the people Gulliver asked the Governor to bring back?
6. What did Gulliver conclude after seeing all those people?
7. Why did Gulliver pretend to be Dutch?
8. How did Gulliver approach the King of Luggnagg? (What was the custom?)
9. Identify Struldbrugs.
10. How do most of the other residents feel about the Struldbrugs?
11. How long had Gulliver been gone on this journey

Book Four I-V
1. How did Gulliver get to the Houyhnhnms' land?
2. What was Gulliver's first reaction to the Yahoos?
3. What did Gulliver conclude about the horses after they finished their first inspection of him?
4. Why was Gulliver's "master" so eager to teach him the language of the Houyhnhnms?
5. What did the word "Houyhnhnm" mean?
6. Why had Gulliver concealed the secret of his dress from the Houyhnhnms?
7. What "human" concept was almost never heard of in the land of the Houyhnhnms?
8. About which part of Gulliver's, (and the human) lifestyle was Gulliver's master most curious?
9. Gulliver discussed the concept of war with his master. What was the master's conclusion?

Book Four VI-IX
1. Why did Gulliver's master think Gulliver was of a noble family?
2. What effect did Gulliver's time with the Houyhnhnms have upon his view of his countrymen?
3. Why did Gulliver go among the Yahoos?
4. How did Gulliver describe the Yahoos?
5. Why did Gulliver feel he could no longer deny he was a real Yahoo?
6. Describe the Houyhnhnms' nature and customs.
7. What is the purpose of the council meeting every fourth year?
8. What question was to be debated at the Grand Assembly while Gulliver was with the Houyhnhnms?
9. What solution to the question did Gulliver's master propose?

Book Four X-XII
1. Gulliver says he could "better endure the sight of a common Yahoo than of my own person." Why could he?
2. Why did Gulliver leave the Houyhnhnms?
3. How did Gulliver feel about his departure?
4. How did Gulliver return to England?
5. What was Gulliver's reaction to his family and countrymen upon his return?
6. What purchases did Gulliver make, and what did he do with them?
7. What was the total length of time that Gulliver traveled?
8. What does Gulliver conclude is the worst vice of mankind?

ANSWER KEY: STUDY GUIDE QUESTIONS *Gulliver's Travels*

Book One - I-IV

1. Who is the narrator, and what does he do for work?
   The narrator is Mr. Lemur Gulliver, and he is the ship's doctor.

2. How did Gulliver get to Lilliput?
   He was aboard the Antelope in the South-Sea when a storm caused the ship to wreck (and subsequently the life boat to overturn). He swam and found land, which he later found was Lilliput.

3. Briefly describe the Lilliputians physical appearance.
   They were very small - only about 6" in height, and everything in Lilliput was scaled proportionally to them.

4. What physical characteristic differentiates the Emperor of Lilliput from his subjects?
   "He is taller by almost a breadth of [Gulliver's] nail than any of his court" . . .

5. What kind of living accommodations did the Emperor provide for Gulliver?
   The Emperor had Gulliver taken to the largest ancient temple in the kingdom. He was chained by the leg, but was able to walk in the courtyard and lie down in the building.

6. The Emperor delivered six Lilliputians who had "attacked" Gulliver to him for justice. What did Gulliver do with them?
   He picked them up and put them in his pocket. One by one he scared them by acting as if he would eat them, then he set them free.

7. When the Lilliputians try to decide what to do with Gulliver what two means of death do they consider before deciding to let him live?
   They consider starvation or shooting him with poisoned arrows.

8. For what purpose do the Lilliputians learn rope dancing and "leaping and creeping"?
   By their performances of these arts, they attempt to impress the Emperor, to gain political offices.

9. Identify Skyresh Bolgolam.
   He is an Admiral of the Realm, advisor to the Emperor, and he disliked Gulliver because he was jealous of him since Gulliver's great capturing of Bolgolam's ships.

10. What were Gulliver's nine conditions of freedom?
    1. Gulliver won't leave without permission.
    2. He won't go into the city without permission and two hours warning to the citizens.
    3. Walk only on high road - not in meadows or fields.
    4. Won't step on anyone or anything and won't pick up people without their permission.
    5. Will carry messenger for Emperor once a month if necessary.
    6. Will be ally of Lilliput against Blefuscu.
    7. Will help with construction and physical labor.
    8. Will survey circumference of Lilliput.
    9. For obedience to above, Gulliver will be fed as much food as 1728 Lilliputians would eat.

11. What are the two political factions in Lilliput?
    The two political factions in Lilliput are the High Heels and the Low Heels. There are more High heels in the country, but the Low Heels are currently in power.

12. About what are the Lilliputians and Blefuscuians fighting?
    Blefuscuians break their eggs on the big end, as was the religious custom until the present Lilliputian Emperor's grandfather decreed eggs should be broken on the small end. Big-Endians (who fled to Blefuscu) and Little-Endians (Lilliputians) have been fighting over which end of the egg to break first.

Book One - V - VIII

1. How did Gulliver help Lilliput against the Blefuscuians?
    He made cables with hooks, crossed the water, hooked the cables to the Blefuscuian ships and pulled them back to Lilliput.

2. The Emperor wanted Gulliver to do more to help him finally crush the Blefuscuians so he could be emperor of all the lands. What was Gulliver's response?
    Gulliver "plainly protested, that [he] would never be an instrument of bringing a free and brave people into slavery."

3. Briefly describe the Lilliputian educational system.
    Children of nobility and means boarded at public nurseries where they were raised and educated with minimum family contact. There were four kinds of nurseries; those being for noble boys, noble girls, ordinary boys and ordinary girls. Children of commons laborers were not educated.

4. Identify Flimnap.
   He is the Lord High Treasurer, Gulliver's "secret enemy" who told the Emperor that His Majesty would eventually go broke paying for Gulliver's food. The treasurer accused Gulliver of having an affair with his wife, (but the accusations were proved false).

5. What crime did the Lilliputians consider to be greater than theft?
   They considered the crime of fraud as being greater than theft.

6. How were citizens who obeyed the laws rewarded?
   Citizens who could prove that they had obeyed the laws for seventy-three moons could claim certain privileges and a monetary reward. They were also given the title of Snilpall, or Legal.

7. What were the Articles of Impeachment against Gulliver?
   1. Gulliver had illegally made water within the precincts of the palace.
   2. Gulliver refused to deliver the Blefuscuians to servitude.
   3. Gulliver was friendly with the Blefuscuians when they came to Lilliput.
   4. Gulliver was preparing for a visit to Blefuscu to see the Emperor of Blefuscu, enemy of the Lilliputian Emperor with only verbal permission to do so.

8. What means of death for Gulliver did the Treasurer and Admiral offer as suggestions?
   (a) Set fire to his house at night - burn him to death and shoot him with poisonous arrows.
   (b) Put poisonous juice on his shirts to make him tear his own flesh.

9. How did the Council decide to punish Gulliver for his crimes?
   They decided to blind him and then starve him to death.

10. How did Gulliver escape?
    He swam to Blefuscu.

11. Why did Gulliver leave Blefuscu?
    The Lilliputian Emperor had demanded his return to Lilliput and although the Blefuscuian Emperor said he would help Gulliver, Gulliver didn't think it proper to put the Blefuscuians in that position. Also Blefuscuians couldn't feed him for long without financial problems.

12. How did Gulliver leave Blefuscu and return to England?
    He found a boat, repaired it, and left. He was picked up by an English merchant vessel run by Capt. John Biddle.

13. In what ways did Gulliver profit financially from his adventure to Lilliput?
    He made a profit from showing small animals and then sold them before he left on his next voyage.

Book Two I - IV

1. How did Gulliver get to Brobdingnag?
   He was sailing on Adventure when stormy weather blew them off course. They spotted land and sent a few men, including Gulliver, to find fresh water. Separated from the others, Gulliver saw them getting into the rowboat, escaping a giant person who was after them.

2. Give a brief physical description of the residents of Brobdingnag.
   They were giants to Gulliver, about 60 feet tall.

3. Who found Gulliver and where did they take him?
   Some laborers found him in a field and took him to the farmer for whom they worked.

4. What "accidents" happened to Gulliver in his first afternoon in the farmer's house?
   The farmer's boy picked him up by the legs and held him upside down. Gulliver discovered that the farmer had cats and dogs, but since he showed no fear of them, they left him alone. The baby picked him up and put Gulliver's head in his mouth. After a nap, Gulliver was attacked by rats, which he killed.

5. Who or what were Grildrig, Glumdalclitch and Splacknuck?
   Grildrig was the name the farmer's daughter gave to Gulliver meaning "Mannikin". Glumdalclitch was the name Gulliver gave the farmer's daughter meaning "little nurse" because she took care of him. Splacknuck is a little animal in Brobdingnag, about 6 feet long.

6. Why did the farmer take Gulliver to market places?
   To show him to the crowds there (for profit.)

7. How did Gulliver meet the Queen?
   A "Gentleman Usher" came from the court to ask the farmer to bring Gulliver for the entertainment of the Queen and her ladies, so the farmer took him.

8. How did Gulliver and Glumdalclitch end up living with the King and Queen?
   The Queen bought Gulliver from the farmer and Gulliver asked the Queen to allow the farmer's daughter to remain with him.

9. Where did Gulliver say the kingdom of Brobdingnag was located?
   Gulliver believed there was a land between Japan and California, and that it joined the northwest parts of America. He thought the kingdom of Brobdingnag was a peninsula that jutted out from this land.

10. What was the Kings' reaction to Gulliver's accounts of English manners, religion, laws and government?
   He fell into a hearty fit of laughing, and "observed how contemptible a thing was human grandeur, which could be mimicked by such diminutive insects as [Gulliver]."

11. Why was the Queen's dwarf mean to Gulliver?
   There was finally someone smaller than him whom he could bully, and he was jealous of the Queen's attention to Gulliver.

12. How was Gulliver transported during his stay in Brobdingnag?
   He was transported in a wooden box, or closet, that was twelve feet square and ten feet high. He had furniture in the closet, and traveled in relative comfort.

Book Two - V - VIII

1. What "ridiculous and troublesome accidents" happened to Gulliver?
   a. Dwarf shook apples down from the tree onto Gulliver.
   b. He was beaten by hailstones.
   c. Spaniel carried the box to the gardener.
   d. The Kite made a swoop at him.
   e. He broke his right shin on a snail shell.

2. Why did Gulliver ask Glumdalclitch not to take him to the Maids of Honor anymore?
   They disgusted him, and injured his pride, thinking him of so little consequence that they were not ashamed to do their toiletries in front of him.

3. What did the monkey do to Gulliver?
   The monkey picked him up and ran off with him, treating him as a young one of its own species.

4. Why did Gulliver attempt to jump over the cow dung, and what happened?
   He wanted exercise, but more importantly it was a point of pride - as a schoolboy attempts to jump over a puddle. Gulliver landed in the dung and was cleaned by a footman with a handkerchief.

5. How did Gulliver attempt to please the King and Queen - and why did he do it?
   a. He made cane chairs and a purse from the Queen's hair.
   b. He played a tune on the spinet which he did to try to restore his pride, so they would think better of him.

6. After Gulliver took great pride in telling the King about England over the period of about a week, what was the King's reaction?
>"I cannot but conclude that the bulk of your natives to be the most pernicious race of little odious vermin that nature ever suffered to crawl upon the surface of the earth."

7. What gift did Gulliver wish to give to the King (so the King would have a more favorable impression of him)? What was the King's reaction?
>Gulliver wanted to show him how to make and use gunpowder. The King was shocked by the uses of gunpowder and wanted nothing to do with it.

8. What was Gulliver's opinion of the learning of the people of Brobdingnag?
>He thought it was defective, because it consisted only of morality, history, poetry, and mathematics. They had no concept of the use of ideas, entities, abstractions, and transcendentals.

9. How long did Gulliver stay in Brobdingnag?
>He stayed there for two years.

10. How did Gulliver leave Brobdingnag, and get back to England?
>A large bird carried his house box out to sea and dropped it there. Captain Wilcock's ship picked him up and took him home.

11. What was the Captain's, and then Gulliver's wife's reaction to his behavior when they first encountered him after his journey?
>They thought he had lost his wits.

Book Three - I - V

1. How did Gulliver get to Laputa?
>He set out on the Hopewell as ship's surgeon on a trip to the East Indies. A storm drove them off course and pirates took the ship. Pirates were going to kill him but instead set him adrift in a canoe. He found some islands and looked to them for survival.

2. On what bizarre object did Gulliver find people?
>On an island which appeared to be floating and maneuverable.

3. Briefly describe the people Gulliver saw.
>Their heads were all inclined either to the right or the left; one of their eyes were turned inward, the other directly up to the Zenith. Their outer garments were adorned with the figures of suns, moons, and stars, interwoven with those of fiddles, flutes, harps, trumpets, guitars, harpsichords, and many other instruments of music, unknown to us in Europe.

4. Identify the use of a flapper.
   A flapper was a servant. The people of Laputa got so engrossed with thinking that their servants would have to hit them with a bladder full of pebbles to draw their attention back to matters at hand.

5. In what way was Gulliver's first meal in Laputa odd?
   The food items were all in geometric shapes.

6. Why didn't Gulliver's new, tailor-made clothes fit?
   The tailor calculated his height and then using mathematics calculated the approximate size of his clothes instead of taking many measurements. The tailor had made an error in his calculations.

7. How did Gulliver describe the Laputians?
   "I have not seen a more clumsy, awkward, and unhappy people, nor so slow and perplexed in their conceptions upon all other subjects, except those of mathematics and music. They are bad reasoners, and vehemently given to opposition, unless when they happen to be of the right opinion, which is seldom the case. Imagination, fancy and invention, they are wholly strangers to; ...the whole compass of their thoughts and mind being shut up within the two aforementioned sciences."

8. Describe the lifestyle of the women who lived on the island.
   The wives and daughters were confined to the island, because the men are afraid that if the women see the rest oft he world, they will not return to the island. They do, however, "live in the greatest plenty and magnificence."

9. The King has two methods of keeping his towns obedient. What are they?
   The first is to keep the island on such a course where they will be deprived of sun and rain, and "consequently afflict the inhabitants with dearth and diseases. And if the crime deserves it, they are at the same time pelted from above with great stones . . ."The second would be "by letting the island drop directly on their heads, which makes a universal destruction both of houses and men."

10. Identify Munodi.
    Munodi was the friends of the lord of the court who had befriended Gulliver. He lived in the city of Lagado and was Gulliver's host while Gulliver remained in that city.

11. How and why were Munodi's lands and home different from others in the area?
    His were well built, well maintained and productive; others were ill-made and unproductive. Munodi believed in the old ways of doing things instead of modern ones.

12. What was the purpose of the Academy of Projectors?
   People who had been to the floating island learned a little about math and science and became dissatisfied with life on the ground when they returned. They began the Academy as a way of "putting arts, sciences, languages and mechanics on a new foot." In the Academy, professors think of new ways of doing things.

13. What's the problem with the Academy?
   The ideas developed there don't work and the real world outside the Academy is going to ruins because the new schemes don't work.

14. What were some of the projects Gulliver saw Professors attempting at the Academy?
   a. One professor was trying to extract sunbeams from cucumbers.
   b. One professor was trying to reduce human excrement to its original food.
   c. One was trying to turn calcine ice into gunpowder.
   d. One was making a method for building houses from the roof down.
   e. A blind professor was teaching apprentices how to distinguish colors by feeling and smelling.
   f. One professor was ploughing fields with hogs instead of a plough.
   g. One was breeding spiders and silkworms to give different colored threads.
   h. One was a doctor who tried to cure ailments with bellows.
   i. One was breeding naked sheep.

15. What common characteristics did these projects have?
   All the projects were essentially ridiculous and were the product of invention for the sake of invention.

16. How were the professors trying to improve the language of the country?
   One project was to shorten polysyllabic words to one syllable, and to leave out verbs and participles. Another was to abolish all words and have men carry the things they needed, and show them to others, instead of talking about them.

Book Three VI - XI
1. What did Gulliver think of the things the political projectors were proposing, and why?
   He called them "wild impossible chimaeras", because they were things which should be done in the world but due to human nature, probably never would be.

2. Why did Gulliver want to go to Luggnagg?
   From there he could find a ship to Japan, and there to find a ship towards England.

3. Why did Gulliver go to Glubbdubdrib?
   He had extra time while waiting for a ship to Luggnagg.

4. What unusual power does the Governor of Glubbdubdrib have?
   He can call up persons from the dead and command their service for no more than 24 hours.

5. Who were some of the people Gulliver asked the Governor to bring back?
   Alexander the Great, Hannibal, Caesar, Pompey, Brutus, [the senate of Rome, a modern parliamentary body], Aristotle, Descartes, Gassendi, and many persons from modern history.

6. What did Gulliver conclude after seeing all those people?
   "It gave [me] melancholy reflections to observe how much the race of human kind was degenerate among us, within these hundred years past".

7. Why did Gulliver pretend to be Dutch?
   "I knew the Dutch were the only Europeans permitted to enter [Japan]."

8. How did Gulliver approach the King of Luggnagg? (What was the custom?
   He had to crawl on his belly and kick the floor as he advanced towards the King. At four yards from the throne he had to rise to his knees, strike his head on the floor seven times and repeat a phrase of greeting.

9. Identify Struldbrugs.
   They are immortals who live in Luggnagg. They live normal lives until the age of thirty. Then they loose affection for life, turn morose, vain, opinionative and peevish. At the age of eighty they are legally dead.

10. How did most of the other residents feel about the Struldbrugs?
    The Struldbrugs are deprived and hated by most of the others.

11. How long had Gulliver been on this journey?
    He had been gone on this journey for five years and six months.

Book Four I-V
1. How did Gulliver get to the Houyhnhnms' land?
   He was the captain of the *Adventure*. After picking up new recruits in Barbados, there was a mutiny on board, which eventually led to Gulliver's being set ashore.

2. What was Gulliver's first reaction to the Yahoos, the first animals he encountered?
   "I never beheld in all my travels so disagreeable an animal, nor one against which I naturally conceived so strong an antipathy."

3. What did Gulliver conclude about the horses after they finished their first inspection of him?

". . . I concluded they must needs be magicians, who had thus metamorphosised themselves. . ."

4. Why was Gulliver's "master" so eager to teach him the language of the Houyhnhnms?

He wanted to learn about Gulliver. He was astonished at the way this Yahoo could imitate rational creatures, and he wanted to understand Gulliver.

5. What did the word "Houyhnhnm" mean?

In English, it translates to "horse," but the derivation of the word in the Houyhynhnm language means "the perfection of nature."

6. Why had Gulliver concealed the secret of his dress from the Houyhnhnms?

He realized that without his clothes, he looked much more like a Yahoo, the creatures he detested.

7. What "human concept was almost never head of in the land of the Houyhnhnms?

The concept of lying or false representation, which the Houyhnhnms called "the thing which was not." was almost never heard of in the land of the Houyhnhnms.

8. About which part of Gulliver's (and the human) lifestyle was Gulliver's master most curious?

He was most curious about the presence and treatment of horses in human society.

9. Gulliver discussed the concept of war with his master. What was the master's conclusion?

". . . But when a creature pretending to reason could be capable of such enormities, he dreaded lest the corruption of that faculty might be worse than brutality itself. He seemed therefore confident, that instead of reason, we were only possessed of some quality fitted to increase our natural vices; as the reflection from a troubled stream returns the image of an ill-shapen body, not only larger, but more distorted.

<u>Book Four VI-IX</u>

1. Why did Gulliver's master think Gulliver was of a noble family?

". . . my master. . . was pleased to make me a compliment which I could not pretend to deserve; that he was sure I must have been born of some noble family, because I far exceeded in shape, colour, and cleanliness, all the Yahoos of his nation, although I seemed to fail in strength and agility, which must be imputed to my different way of living from those other brutes; and besides, I was not only endowed with the faculty of speech, but likewise with some rudiments of reason, to a degree that with all his acquaintances I passed for a prodigy.

2. What effect did Gulliver's time with the Houyhnhnms have upon his view of his countrymen?

" . . . the many virtues of those excellent quadrupeds placed in opposite view to human corruptions, had so far opened my eyes and enlarged my understanding, that I began to view the actions and passions of man in a very different light, and to think the honor of my own kind not worth managing. . . ."

3. Why did Gulliver go among the Yahoos?

He went to observe them (and probably secretly hoping to find more differences between him and them.)

4. How did Gulliver describe the Yahoos?

They were nimble and good swimmers from infancy. They had a rank smell. He thought them to be unteachable, yet cunning, malicious, treacherous, and revengeful.

5. Why did Gulliver feel he could no longer deny he was a real Yahoo?

A Yahoo female showed her attraction for him at the river. He thought that since she was attracted to him, he must be a Yahoo. He did not take into account the equally important fact that he was not at all attracted to her.

6. Describe the Houyhnhnms' nature and customs.

"As these noble Houyhnhnms are endowed by nature with a general disposition to all virtues, and have no conceptions or ideas of what is evil in a rational creature, so their grand maxim is to cultivate reason, and to be wholly governed by it. . . So that controversies, wranglings, disputes, and positiveness in false or dubious propositions, are evils unknown among the Houyhnhnms. Friendship and benevolence are the two principal virtues among the Houyhnhnms. They preserve decency and civility in the highest degrees. . . The married pair pass their lives with the same friendship and mutual benevolence that they bear to all others of the same species who come in their way; without jealousy, fondness, quarreling, or discontent. Temperance, industry, exercise and cleanliness, are the lessons equally enjoined to the young ones of both sexes. . . "

7. What is the purpose of the council meeting every fourth year?

"Every fourth year, at the vernal equinox, there is a representative council of the whole nation, which meets in a plain about twenty miles from our house, and continues about five or six days. Here they enquire into the state and condition of the several districts; whether they abound or be deficient in hay or oats, or cows or Yahoos. And wherever there is any want (which is seldom) it is immediately supplied by unanimous consent and contribution. Here likewise the regulation of children is settled: as for instance, if a Houyhnhnm hath two males, he changeth one of them with another that hath two females; and when a child hath been lost by casualty, where the mother is past breeding, it is determined what family in the district shall breed another to supply the loss.

8. What question was to be debated at the Grand Assembly while Gulliver was with the Houyhnhnms?
    They were debating whether the Yahoos should be exterminated from the face of the earth.

9. What solution to the question did Gulliver's master propose?
    He proposed that the young males be castrated (after hearing the description of the treatment of male horses from Gulliver.) That way, the Yahoos would eventually die off, and the Houyhnhnms could not be accountable for destroying life.

Book Four X-XII

1. Gulliver says he could "better endure the sight of a common Yahoo than of my own person." Why could he?
    Yahoos had vices, but men also had reason, which they inappropriately used to increase their natural vices. He was ashamed to be a man.

2. Why did Gulliver have to leave the Houyhnhnms?
    Even though Gulliver was better than the average Yahoo by means of his ability to reason and converse, he was still a possible source of problems for the Houyhnhnms. His master would have him stay, but the others demanded his departure.

3. How did Gulliver feel about his departure?
    He was "struck with he utmost grief and despair," and fainted at his master's feet.

4. How did Gulliver return to England?
    He made a canoe which took him to some islands where natives shot him in the knee with an arrow. He moved to another part of the island. There some Europeans found him and took him home, thinking he had gone crazy. They treated him with great kindness.

5. What was Gulliver's reaction to his family and countrymen upon his return?
    He rejected them.

6. What purchases did Gulliver make after he returned home, and what did he do with them?
    He bought two horses, hired a groom, and spent several hours each day conversing with the horses.

7. What was the total length of time that Gulliver traveled?
    He traveled for sixteen years and seven months.

8. What does Gulliver conclude is the worst vice of mankind?
    He decides that pride is man's worst vice.

STUDY GUIDE QUESTIONS MULTIPLE CHOICE FORMAT *Gulliver's Travels*

Book One-I-IV

1. How is the story told?
    a. It is told in the first person by the ship's doctor.
    b. It is told in the second person in the form of letters from the first mate to his wife.
    c. It is told in the third person by a nephew of the traveler.
    d. It is told through the diary of the ship's captain.

2. True or False: Gulliver got to Lilliput when the ship he was on was wrecked and the lifeboat overturned.
    a. True
    b. False

3. What did the Lilliputians look like?
    a. They were about 24" high.
    b. They were about 6" high.
    c. They were about 15" high.
    d. They were about 3" high.

4. What physical characteristic differentiates the Emperor of Lilliput from his subjects?
    a. He is the only person with brown hair.
    b. He has six toes on each foot.
    c. He is taller than anyone else.
    d. He is the strongest person in the country.

5. What kind of living accommodations did the Emperor provide for Gulliver?
    a. The Emperor had Gulliver taken to the largest ancient temple in the kingdom.
    b. The people erected a large tent for him in the middle of the town square.
    c. He was taken to the wilderness and chained to a tree.
    d. He was given a pen in the stables with the animals.

6. The Emperor delivered six Lilliputians who had attacked Gulliver to him for justice. What did he do with them?
    a. He threw them as far as he could, forcing them to walk all the way back to Lilliput.
    b. He put them in his pocket and pretended to eat them. Then he set them free.
    c. He gave them back to the Emperor and said he would abide by whatever course of action the Emperor wanted.
    d. He forced them to be his servants for day. They had to bring his food, comb his hair, and give him a bath.

7. When the Lilliputians try to decide what to do with Gulliver what two means of death do they consider before deciding to let him live?
   a. They consider poisoning his food or suffocating him.
   b. They consider drowning or starvation.
   c. They consider setting him on fire or shooting him.
   d. They consider starvation or shooting him with poisoned arrows.

8. For what purpose do the Lilliputians learn rope dancing and "leaping and creeping?"
   a. They learn it to keep fit. in case of an attack from an enemy.
   b. They attempt to impress the Emperor, to gain political offices.
   c. They could earn a great deal of money as entertainers.
   d. They think it keeps away the evil spirits.

9. Which of the following does not describe Skyresh Bolgolam?
   a. He is the Emperor's nephew.
   b. He is jealous of Gulliver
   c. He is an Admiral of the Realm.
   d. Gulliver captured his ships.

10. Which of the following was **not** one of Gulliver's conditions of freedom?
    a. He won't leave without permission.
    b. He must give the citizens two hours' warning before entering the city.
    c. He must wear a bell around his neck so the people will hear him coming.
    d. He must walk only on the high road, not in meadows or fields.

11. True or False: Another one of the conditions of freedom was that Gulliver would be an ally of Lilliput against the Blefuscuians.
    a. True
    b. False

12. How much food did Gulliver eat?
    a. He ate as much as a herd of their cattle.
    b. He ate an entire storage barn's worth every day.
    c. He ate twelve tons.
    d. He ate as much as 1728 Lilliputians.

13. What are the two political factions in Lilliput?
    a. They are the Pointed Ears and the Rounded Ears.
    b. They are the High Heels and the Low Heels.
    c. They are the Long Hairs and the Short Hairs.
    d. They are the Soft Voices and the Loud Voices.

14. About what are the Lilliputians and the Blefuscuians fighting?
	a. They are fighting over who discovered their respective islands. Each group claims that one of their ancestors was the discoverer.
	b. They are fighting over whether to consolidate and become one large power or to stay two small powers. Opinions are about evenly divided.
	c. They are fighting over which end of the egg to break first. The Lilliputians break theirs on the little end and the Blefuscuians break theirs on the large end.
	d. They are fighting over whether to use their dinner forks in the right or left hand. The Blefuscuians think it proper to hold the fork in the right hand, while the Lilliputians hold it in the left.

Study Guide Questions Multiple Choice Format *Gulliver's Travels*

Book One V-VII

15. How did Gulliver help Lilliput against the Blefuscuians.?
    a. He crossed the water and pulled the Blefuscuian ships to Lilliput.
    b. He built a massive stone wall around the island of Lilliput so no one could get in.
    c. He was tall enough to merely look across the water and spy on the Blefuscuians.
    d. He went to Blefuscuians. and stole all of their money.

16. The Emperor wanted Gulliver to do more to help him finally crush the Blefuscuians so he could be emperor of all the lands. What was Gulliver's response?
    a. He agreed that "The stronger power should claim sovereignty over all the land."
    b. He "Plainly protested that he would never be an instrument of bringing a free and brave people into slavery."
    TWO CHOICES ONLY

17. True or False: Children of nobility and means were boarded and raised at public nurseries with almost no family contact.
    a. True
    b. False

18. How many kinds of nurseries were there?
    a. There were six.
    b. There were five.
    c. There were four.
    d. There were three.

19. True or False: All children were educated: noble, ordinary, and common.
    a. True
    b. False

20. True or False: The Lilliputian tailors used Gulliver's big toe to determine his measurements.
    a. True
    b. False

21. Who is Flimnap?
    a. He is the Secretary of Education. He doesn't want Gulliver to tell the people about the "outside world."
    b. He is the Minister of Internal Affairs. He wants Gulliver to leave Lilliput because he is creating too much disturbance and curiosity.
    c. He is the Chief Medical Administrator. He is afraid Gulliver will contaminate the people with unknown diseases.
    d. He is the Lord High Treasurer. He thinks the Emperor will eventually go broke from paying for Gulliver's food.

22. Which of the following was not one of the Articles of Impeachment against Gulliver?
    a. He had illegally made water within the precincts of the palace.
    b. He refused to deliver the Blefuscuians to servitude.
    c. He tried to seduce the wife of the Minister of Justice.
    d. He was friendly with the Blefuscuians when they came to Lilliput.

23. True or False: The Treasurer and Admiral suggested the following two means of death for Gulliver: Burn him to death and shoot him with poisonous arrows, and put poisonous juice on his shirts to make him tear his own flesh.
    a. True
    b. False

24. How did the Council decide to punish Gulliver?
    a. They decided to banish him.
    b. They decided to blind him and then starve him to death.
    c. They decided to shoot him with poisoned arrows and then break his legs.
    d. They decided to drive him into the sea and drown him.

25. How did Gulliver escape?
    a. He stepped on the armory and destroyed all of their weapons.
    b. He held the Emperor hostage until the Lilliputians agreed to leave him alone.
    c. He swam to Blefuscu.
    d. He stood on top of their highest mountain and threatened to hurl rocks at the town unless they treated him better.

26. True or False: Gulliver left Blefuscu so that he would not put the Blefuscuian Emperor in an awkward position.
    a. True
    b. False

27. True or False: Gulliver was able to leave Blefuscu because he discovered that the ocean was shallow enough for a few miles that he was able to walk through it. Then he swam until he was picked up by an English ship.
 a. True
 b. False

28. In what ways did Gulliver profit from his adventure to Lilliput?
 a. He wrote a book about his adventures and earned a great deal of money in royalties.
 b. He lectured to various groups and was paid well for the lectures.
 c. He had stolen a great deal of gold from both countries and was able to live comfortably on the income.
 d. He made a profit from showing and selling small animals.

Study Guide Questions Multiple Choice Format *Gulliver's Travels*

Book Two-I-IV

29. True or False: Gulliver found an old map that showed a series of small, unexplored islands.
    a. True
    b. False

30. Give a brief physical description of the residents of Brobdingnag.
    a. They were the same size as Gulliver.
    b. They were smaller than Gulliver, but larger than the Lilliputians.
    c. They were about 15 feet tall.
    d. They were giants, about 60 feet tall.

31. Who found Gulliver and where did they take him?
    a. The king's daughter found him and took him to her father.
    b. Some laborers found him and took him to the farmer for whom they worked.
    c. Two young boys took him to their secret clubhouse and hid him
    d. The pastor found him and took him home to the parsonage.

32. What "accident" happened to Gulliver in his first afternoon in his host's house?
    a. He fell off the dining table.
    b. He almost drowned in a cup of water.
    c. The boy picked him up by the legs and held him upside down.
    d. He was bitten by a dog and almost lost his leg.

33. True or False: The baby thought Gulliver was a rattle and almost shook him to death.
    a. True
    b. False

34. True or False: After a nap, Gulliver was attacked by rats, which he killed.
    a. True
    b. False

35. What did the name "Grildrig" mean?
    a. It meant "Traveler."
    b. It meant "Mannikin."
    c. It meant "Handsome Little One."
    d. It meant "Curiosity."

36. What name meaning "little nurse" did Gulliver give the farmer's daughter?
    a. He called her "Grenaldine."
    b. He called her "Sprangligry."
    c. He called her "Glumdalclitch."
    d. He called her "Drildgrig."

37. True or False: Splacknuck is a little animal in Brobdingnay, about 6 feet long.
    a. True
    b. False

38. Why did the farmer take Gulliver to the market places?
    a. He wanted to show him to the crowds there for profit.
    b. He wanted to help Gulliver learn about the customs of the people.
    c. He took Gulliver there to buy the food he wanted to eat.
    d. He was thinking of selling Gulliver to the highest bidder, but he changed his mind.

39. True or False: The farmer asked for an audience with the Queen, hoping that showing Gulliver at court would bring him fame and fortune.
    a. True
    b. False

40. True or False: The Queen bought Gulliver and Gulliver asked the Queen to allow Glumdalclitch to remain with him.
    a. True
    b. False

41. Where did Gulliver say the kingdom of Brobdingnag was located?
    a. He said it was near Australia.
    b. He said it was off the coast of Africa.
    c. He said it was between Japan and California, off the northwest coast of America.
    d. He said it connected China and Europe.

42. What was the King's reaction to Gulliver's accounts of English manners, laws, religion, and government?
    a. He fell into a heart fit of laughing, and "observed how contemptible a thing was human grandeur, which could be mimicked by such diminutive insects as Gulliver
    b. He somberly agreed that "sentient beings, regardless of size, all strove to maintain order and sensibility in their worlds."
    TWO CHOICES ONLY

43. What was the dwarf's reaction to Gulliver?
    a. He pitied the small, helpless-looking creature. He became very protective of Gulliver.
    b. He was jealous of the Queen's attention, and glad to have someone to bully.
    c. It was immediate disgust and distrust.
    d. He wanted to be good friends with Gulliver.

44. How was Gulliver transported during his stay in Brobdingnag?
    a. He rode a bicycle that had been made for him.
    b. He was carried in a wooden box, which he called a closet.
    c. Glumdalclitch carried him in her pocket.
    d. He flew on the back of a dove.

Study Guide Questions Multiple Choice Format *Gulliver's Travels*

Book Two- V-VIII

45. Which was **not** one of the "ridiculous and troublesome accidents" that happened to Gulliver ?
    a. Dwarf shook apples down from the tree onto Gulliver.
    b. He was beaten by hailstones.
    c. He was hit in the leg by a hazelnut.
    d. He was almost smothered when the Kite fell on him.

46. Why did Gulliver ask Glumdalclitch not to take him to the Maids of Honor anymore?
    a. He found their conversation boring.
    b. He was allergic to their perfumes and became quite ill.
    c. They disgusted him and injured his pride by doing their toiletries in front of him.
    d. He didn't like being around so many women. He really wanted to join in the company of the men, but Glumdalclitch was not allowed, and he was afraid to go without her.

Study Guide Questions Multiple Choice Format *Gulliver's Travels*

47. What did the monkey do to Gulliver ?
    a. It tried to eat him.
    b. It picked him up and ran off with him, treating him as a young one of its own species.
    c. It put him up in a tree for safe-keeping, and then would not let him down.
    d. It tried to give him a bath and almost drowned him.

48. What happened when Gulliver tried to jump over the cow dung?
    a. He landed in it and was cleaned by a footman.
    b. He cleared it and felt proud of himself.
    TWO CHOICES ONLY

49. How did Gulliver try to please the King and Queen?
    a. He recited poetry for them.
    b. He taught them an English folk dance.
    c. He sang to them.
    d. He made chairs and a purse from the Queen's hair.

50. After Gulliver took great pride in telling the King about England over the period of about a week, what was the King's reaction?
    a. He asked Gulliver to take him there for a visit.
    b. He said he was glad he was not an Englishman.
    c. He expressed his displeasure with the country and the people.
    d. He felt envious of the superiority of the English.

51. What was Gulliver's opinion of the learning of the people of Brobdingnag?
    a. He thought they were extremely well-rounded.
    b. He thought their education was defective.
    TWO CHOICES ONLY

52. What gift did Gulliver wish to give the King so the King would have a more favorable impression of him?
    a. Gulliver showed him a Bible and offered to teach him to read English.
    b. Gulliver offered him several gold crowns.
    c. Gulliver offered the King a year's worth of service.
    d. Gulliver offered to show the King how to make and use gunpowder.

53. What was the King's reaction?
    a. The King accepted the gift.
    b. The King rejected the gift.

54. How long did Gulliver stay in Brobdingnag?
    a. He stayed there for six months.
    b. He stayed there for twelve years.
    c. He stayed there for two years.
    d. He stayed there for one year and eight months.

55. How did Gulliver leave Brobdingnag and get back to England?
    a. He flew on the Kite and landed in London.
    b. The King ordered his men to make a ship for Gulliver, and he sailed home.
    c. A large bird carried his house box out to sea and dropped it. Then he was picked up by an English ship.
    d. One of the giants carried him through the sea to a location close to England. Gulliver then started swimming, and was picked up by a Spanish vessel. The captain took him to Spain, and he then traveled overland to England.

56. What was the Captain's, and then Gulliver's wife's reaction to his behavior when they first encountered him after his journey?
    a. They thought he had lost his wits.
    b. They thought he had learned a lot.
    c. They thought he was just the same as when he left.
    d. They thought his disposition was much improved.

Study Guide Questions Multiple Choice Format *Gulliver's Travels*

Book Three I-V

57. True or False: While Gulliver was on the Hopewell, it was attacked by pirates. They set him adrift in a canoe and he landed on the island of Laputa.
    a. True
    b. False

58. On what bizarre object did Gulliver find people?
    a. They were on an island which appeared to be floating and maneuverable.
    b. They were on a giant piece of fruit.
    c. They were on the back of a giant turtle.
    d. They were on a large piece of driftwood.

59. Which of the following statement describes the people Gulliver saw?
    a. They had two eyes on each side of their heads, but no mouths.
    b. Their heads were all inclined either to the right or to the left; one eye was turned inward, and the other was turned directly up.
    c. They had very long ear lobes, three nostrils, and teeth that protruded over their lips.
    d. Their facial features were the same on the front and the back, so that it was possible to talk to both sides of the person at the same time.

60. What did their clothes look like?
    a. They were made of a translucent material that Gulliver had never seen before.
    b. They didn't wear any clothes.
    c. They dressed exactly like the English of the Twelfth century.
    d. They had figures of suns and moons interwoven with musical instruments.

61. What was the use of a flapper?
    a. The flapper was a large leaf that was use as a fan and to keep away the many irritating bugs that grew on the island.
    b. The people were very hard of hearing. The flapper was placed behind the ear to catch the speaker's words and channel them into the listener's ear.
    c. The flapper was a servant. The servant would hit the Laputians with bladder full of pebbles tied to a stick, to focus their attention.
    d. The people were very quarrelsome, and couldn't gather in groups of more than two. The flappers were police who used large sticks with fans at either end to keep people apart.

62. What was odd about Gulliver's first meal in Laputa?
    a. He discovered that the people ate only fruit for breakfast, meat for lunch, and sweets for dinner. He arrived in time for dinner so all he was given was pastries and candies.
    b. None of the food was cooked.
    c. Everything was in geometric shapes.
    d. The people ate standing on their heads.

63. Why didn't Gulliver's clothes fit?
    a. No one there knew how to sew, and they weren't able to clothe him correctly.
    b. The tailor had made an error in his mathematical calculations.
    c. Gulliver refused to stand still and have them fitted, so the seamstress had to guess at his size.
    d. He had lost a great deal of weight, and his clothes were too big.

64. Which of the following does not describe the Laputians?
    a. They were clumsy, awkward and unhappy.
    b. They were bad reasoners.
    c. They were vehemently given to opposition.
    d. They were very weak in mathematic and musical abilities.

65. True or False: The women who lived on the island were allowed to travel anywhere in the kingdom whenever they wanted to.
    a. True
    b. False

66. True or False: The King kept the island on a course so that the people were deprived of sun and rain, and constantly afflicted with dearth and diseases.
    a. True
    b. False

67. True or False: If the people were disobedient, the King made them swim behind the island.
    a. True
    b. False

68. Who was Munodi?
    a. He was the secretary to the King.
    b. He was the scientist who developed the plan for the island.
    c. He was the friend of the lord of the court, and was Gulliver's host.
    d. He was the King's second cousin, and heir to the throne. He secretly wanted to get rid of the King, and was thinking of ways to get Gulliver to help him do so.

69. How were Munodi's lands and home different from the others in the area?
    a. His were twice the size of everyone else's.
    b. His were antiquated, without the modern conveniences of his neighbors.
    c. His home was filled with art works and expensive furniture. His lands were covered with landscaped gardens
    d. His were well built, well maintained, and productive.

70. Some of the people who had been to the floating island learned a little about math and science and became satisfied with life on the ground when they returned. They began an institution "to put arts, sciences, languages, and mechanics on a new foot." What was the institution called?
    a. It was called "The Institute for Learning."
    b. It was called "The Land Dwellers' University."
    c. It was called "The School for the Sciences and the Arts."
    d. It was called "The Academy of Projectors."

71. True or False: The ideas developed at the special institution didn't work, and the real world outside was going to ruins because of this.
    a. True
    b. False

72. Which of the following was not one of the projects Gulliver saw the Professors attempting?
    a. One professor was trying to extract sunbeams from cucumbers.
    b. One professor was trying to reduce human excrement to its original food.
    c. One professor was trying to turn calcium carbonate into paper that could be written on and then eaten.
    d. One professor was making a method for building houses from the roof down.

73. True or False: A blind professor had developed a special hearing aid that allowed its wearer to "hear" colors.
    a. True
    b. False

74. Which of the following was not one of the projects Gulliver saw professors attempting?
    a. One professor was teaching math by writing on a wafer and having his students eat the wafer.
    b. One professor was ploughing fields with hogs instead of a plough.
    c. One professor was working to abolish the use of words, in an effort to save the lungs.
    d. One professor was breeding sheep who had wool of different colors.

75. True or False: The projects were sensible and were actually making a difference in the quality of life of the people.
    a. True
    b. False
76. How were the professors trying to improve the language of the country?
    a. They were turning all spoken language into songs.
    b. They were reducing all polysyllabic words to words with one syllable, and doing away with verbs and participles.
    c. They were developing a picture language to be used along with spoken language.
    d. They were going to have Gulliver teach everyone to speak English, and then forbid the use of their own language.

Study Guide Questions Multiple Choice Format *Gulliver's Travels*

Book Three-VI-XI

77. True or False: Gulliver called the political propositions "chimaeras" because they were such good, workable ideas.
    a. True
    b. False

78. Why did Gulliver go to Luggnagg?
    a. He was taken there against his will by the captain of the boat.
    b. He wanted to write a book about the country.
    c. He would be able to find a ship to Japan, and then find a ship to England.
    d. He thought he could become the ruler, because he and heard there was inner turmoil and the people wanted a strong leader.

79. Why did Gulliver go to Glubbdubdrib?
    a. His ship was blown off course.
    b. He stopped there to get fruit and vegetables.
    c. He had an inaccurate map and landed there by mistake.
    d. He had time to kill while waiting for a ship to Luggnagg.

80. Who had the unusual power of calling up persons from the dead?
    a. It was the Archbishop.
    b. It was the Governor.
    c. It was the Head Sorceress.
    d. It was the oldest person on the island.

81. Which of the following people was **not** brought back at Gulliver's request?
    a. Alexander the Great
    b. Aristotle
    c. Gandhi
    d. Caesar

82. What did Gulliver conclude after seeing all those people?
    a. Humans had made advances within the last hundred years.
    b. Humans had degenerated within the last hundred years."
    TWO CHOICES ONLY

83. What nationality did Gulliver pretend to be, since they were the only Europeans permitted to enter Japan?
    a. He pretended to be Dutch.
    b. He pretended to be German.
    c. He pretended to be Swedish.
    d. He pretended to be French.

84. True or False: To approach the King of Luggnagg, one had to crawl on his belly and kick the floor as he advanced towards the King. At four yards from the throne he had to rise to his knees, strike his head on the floor seven times and repeat a phrase of greeting.
    a. True
    b. False

85. True or False: The Struldbrugs lived an accelerated life, aging the equivalent of ten years in one. They then died at age thirty.
    a. True
    b. False

86. How did most of the other residents feel about the Struldbrugs?
    a. They envied their immortality.
    b. They hated the Struldbrugs.
    c. Most of the people felt compassion towards them and their unusual circumstances.
    d. Since the identities of the Struldbrugs were kept secret, most people didn't even know who they were, and so ignored them.

87. How long had Gulliver been gone on this journey?
    a. He had been gone for five years and six months.
    b. He had been gone for ten and a half months.
    c. He had been gone for exactly one year.
    d. He had been gone for two years and three days.

Study Guide Questions Multiple Choice Format *Gulliver's Travels*

Book Four I-V

88. How did Gulliver get to the Houyhnhnms' land?
    a. The ship he was on was blown off course.
    b. The captain wanted to show the island to Gulliver, so he set out there deliberately.
    c. There was a mutiny on board the ship, and Gulliver was set ashore there.
    d. Gulliver had been told about the land, and had asked to go there.

89. What was Gulliver's first reaction to the Yahoos, the first animals he encountered?
    a. He thought they were disagreeable.
    b. He thought they were very attractive.
    c. He thought they were mysterious.
    d. He thought they were funny and entertaining.

90. What did Gulliver conclude about the horses after they finished their first inspection of him?
    a. He thought they were magicians.
    b. He thought they were devils.
    c. He thought they were smelly savages.
    d. He thought they were gods.

91. Why was Gulliver's "master" so eager to teach him the language of the Houyhnhnms?
    a. He wanted Gulliver to be able to teach him to speak English.
    b. He wanted to train Gulliver to perform menial tasks.
    c. He wanted to learn about Gulliver, and to understand him.
    d. He wanted to learn where Gulliver came from, because he wanted to send an army there to conquer the people.

92. What was the derivation of the word "Houyhnhnm" according to their language?
    a. It meant "beast of burden."
    b. It meant "one who walks on four legs."
    c. It meant "of great intelligence."
    d. It meant "the perfection of nature."

93. True or False: Gulliver concealed the secret of his dress from the Houyhnhnms because he was afraid they would steal his clothes to study them. (Book Four I-V)
    a. True
    b. False

94. Gulliver and his master had several discussions. To what subject does the following quotation refer? "...But when a creature pretending to reason could be capable of such enormities, he dreaded lest the corruption of that faculty might be worse than brutality itself. He seemed therefore confident that instead of reason, we were only possessed of some quality fitted to increase our natural vices: as the reflection from a troubled stream returns the image of an ill-shapen body, not only larger, but more distorted."
    a. They were discussing the concept of sin.
    b. They were discussing the concept of war.
    c. They were discussing the concept of money.
    d. They were discussing the concept of death.

Study Guide Questions Multiple Choice Format *Gulliver's Travels*

Book Four VI-IX

95. What did Gulliver's master think of him?
    a. He thought Gulliver was of a noble family.
    b. He thought Gulliver was from hearty peasant stock.
    TWO CHOICES ONLY

96. What effect did Gulliver's time with the Houyhnhnms have upon his view of his countrymen?
    a. He began to thing they were not as honorable as he had once thought.
    b. He thought even more highly of them than he had previously.
    TWO CHOICES ONLY

97. True or False: Gulliver went among the Yahoos to observe them and try to find more differences between him and them.
    a. True
    b. False

98. Why did Gulliver feel he could no longer deny he was a real Yahoo?
    a. He enjoyed the same food as they did.
    b. He preferred their company to that of the Houyhnhnms
    c. A female Yahoo showed her attraction to him.
    d. His thoughts and actions were similar to theirs.

99. Which of the following does not describe the Houyhnhnms' nature and customs?
    a. The have a virtuous disposition.
    b. They believe in friendship.
    c. They preserve decency and civility.
    d. They are ruled by emotion.

100. What is the purpose of the council meeting every fourth year?
    a. They meet to plan a banquet.
    b. They meet to enquire into the condition of the districts.
    c. They meet to collect taxes.
    d. They meet to elect new officials.

101. What question was to be debated at the Grand Assembly while Gulliver was with the Houyhnhnms?
    a. They were debating where to build a new palace.
    b. They were debating whether or not to make contact with the Europeans.
    c. They were debating whether or not to exterminate the entire race of Yahoos.
    d. They were debating whether or not to make Gulliver an honorary Houyhnhnm.

102. True or False: Gulliver's master proposed that all young male Yahoos be castrated.
    a. True
    b. False

Study Guide Questions Multiple Choice Format *Gulliver's Travels*

<u>Book Four X-XII</u>

103. How did Gulliver feel about humans after observing the Yahoos?
    a. He felt that humans were far superior to the Yahoos.
    b. He was ashamed to be a man.
    TWO CHOICES ONLY

104. Why did Gulliver have to leave the Houyhnhnms?
    a. He was running out of money.
    b. He was ill, and knew that only a human doctor could help him.
    c. The Houyhnhnms demanded it.
    d. He was eager to have a new adventure.

105. How did Gulliver feel about his departure?
    a. He was glad to leave.
    b. He was very sad to be leaving.

106. True or False: Gulliver returned to England by riding one of the Houyhnhnms overland.
    a. True
    b. False

107. What was Gulliver's reaction to his family and countrymen upon his return?
    a. He embraced them and vowed never to leave again.
    b. He rejected them.

108. What purchases did Gulliver make?
    a. He bought new clothes and shoes.
    b. He bought a ship in case he wanted to go back to sea.
    c. He bought one of the newest globes so that he could look for the lands he had visited.
    d. He bought two horses.

109. What was the total length of time that Gulliver had traveled?.
    a. He had traveled for thirty years.
    b. He had traveled for seven years and eleven months.
    c. He had traveled for twenty-three years, eight months, and nineteen days.
    d. He had traveled for sixteen years and seven months.

110. What does Gulliver conclude is the worst vice of mankind?
	a. He concludes that it is greed.
	b. He concludes that it is deception.
	c. He concludes that it is pride.
	d. He concludes that it is lust.

ANSWER KEY MULTIPLE CHOICE STUDY QUESTIONS *Gulliver's Travels*

1.	a.	38.	a.	75.	b. False
2.	a. True	39.	b. False	76.	b.
3.	b.	40.	a. True	77.	b. False
4.	c.	41.	c.	78.	c.
5.	a.	42.	a.	79.	d.
6.	b.	43.	b.	80.	b.
7.	d.	44.	b.	81.	c.
8.	b.	45.	c.	82.	b.
9.	a.	46.	c.	83.	a.
10.	c.	47.	b.	84.	a. True
11.	a. True	48.	a.	85.	b. False
12.	d.	49.	d.	86.	b.
13.	b.	50.	b.	87.	a.
14.	c.	51.	b.	88.	c.
15.	a.	52.	d.	89.	a.
16.	b.	53.	b.	90.	a.
17.	a. True	54.	c.	91.	c.
18.	c.	55.	c.	92.	d.
19.	b. False	56.	a.	93.	b. False
20.	b. False	57.	a. True	94.	b.
21.	d.	58.	a.	95.	a.
22.	c.	59.	b.	96.	a.
23.	a. True	60.	d.	97.	a. True
24.	b.	61.	c.	98.	c.
25.	c.	62.	c.	99.	d.
26.	a. True	63.	b.	100.	b.
27.	b. False	64.	a.	101.	c.
28.	d.	65.	b. False	102.	a.
29.	b. False	66.	a. True	103.	b.
30.	d.	67.	b. False	104.	c.
31.	b.	68.	c.	105.	b.
32.	c.	69.	d.	106.	b. False
33.	b. False	70.	d.	107.	b.
34.	a. True	71.	a. True	108.	d.
35.	b.	72.	c.	109.	d.
36.	c.	73.	b. False	110.	c.
37.	a. True	74.	d.		

VOCABULARY PREREADING WORKSHEETS

Vocabulary *Gulliver's Travels* Part One Chapters I-IV

Part One
Chapters I - IV Part I: Using Prior Knowledge and Contextual Clues

Below are the sentences in which the vocabulary words appear in the text. Read the sentence. Use any clues you can find in the sentence combined with your prior knowledge, and write what you think the underlined words mean on the lines provided.

1. We rowed, by my computation, about three **leagues**.

_____

2. The **declivity** was so small that I walked near a mile before I got to the shore.

_____

3. . . . being a most ingenious people, they slung up with great dexterity one of their largest **hogsheads**, then rolled it towards my hand, and beat out the top; I drank it off at a draught, which I might well do, for it did not hold half a pint.

_____

4., 5., 6. However, in my thoughts I could not sufficiently wonder at the **intrepidity** of these **diminutive** mortals, who durst venture to mount and walk upon my body, while one of my hands was at liberty, without trembling at the very sight of so **prodigious** a creature as I must appear to them.

_____

_____

7. I treated the rest in the same manner, taking them one by one out of my pocket, and I observed both the soldiers and people were highly obliged at this mark of my **clemency**, which was represented very much to my advantage at court.

_____

Vocabulary *Gulliver's Travels* Part One Chapters I-IV continued

8. ... his Majesty's mathematicians, having taken the height of my body by the help of a **quadrant**, and finding it to exceed theirs in the proportion of twelve to one, concluded ... that mine must contain at least 1728 of theirs.

_____

9. The **animosities** between these two parties run so high that they will neither eat not drink, nor talk with each other.

_____

10. ... the Emperors of Blefuscu did frequently **expostulate** by their ambassadors, accusing us of making a schism in religion, by offending against a fundamental doctrine of our great prophet Lustrog.

_____

Part II: Determining the Meaning   Match the vocabulary words to their dictionary definitions.

____ 1. leagues   A. mercy
____ 2. declivity   B. to reason earnestly with someone
____ 3. hogshead   C. bitter hostilities, hatred
____ 4. intrepidity   D. sloping downward
____ 5. diminutive   E. a square; the quarter of a circle; a navigation instrument
____ 6. prodigious   F. courage, fearlessness
____ 7. clemency   G. extraordinary size, amount, etc.; abnormal
____ 8. quadrant   H. a large cask
____ 9. animosities   I. small, tiny
____ 10. expostulate   J. units of distance, each equal to three miles

Vocabulary *Gulliver's Travels* Part One Chapters V - VIII

Part I: Using Prior Knowledge and Contextual Clues

Below are the sentences in which the vocabulary words appear in the text. Read the sentence. Use any clues you can find in the sentence combined with your prior knowledge, and write what you think the underlined words mean on the lines provided.

1. My greatest apprehension was for my eyes, which I should have infallibly lost, if I had not suddenly thought of an **expedient**. I kept, among other little necessaries, a pair of spectacles, in a private pocket.

_____

2, 3. . . . but if the person accused maketh his innocence plainly to appear upon his trial, the accuser is immediately put to an **ignominious** death; and out of his goods or lands, the innocent person is quadruply **recompensed** for the loss of time, for the danger he underwent, for the hardship of his imprisonment, and for all the charges he hath been at in making his defense.

_____

_____

4. The image of Justice, in their courts of judicature, is formed with six eyes, two before, as many behind, and on each side one, to signify **circumspection**. . . to show she is more disposed to reward than to punish.

_____

5. After the common salutations were over, observing his Lordship's **countenance** full of concern, and enquiring into the reason, he desired I would hear him with patience in a matter that highly concerned my honour and my life.

_____

6. This Lord, in conjunction with Flimnap, . . . have prepared Articles of **Impeachment** against you, for treason, and other capital crimes.

_____

7. This proposal was received with the utmost **disapprobation** by the whole board.

_____

Vocabulary *Gulliver's Travels* Part One Chapters V - VIII Continued

8. I sometimes thought of standing my trial, for although I could not deny the facts alleged in the several articles, yet I hoped they would admit of some **extenuations**.

_____

9. . . . because if I had then known the nature of princes and ministers, . . . and their methods of treating criminals, I should with great **alacrity** and readiness have submitted to so easy a punishment.

_____

10. I stayed but two months with my wife and family, for my **insatiable** desire of seeing foreign countries would suffer me to continue no longer.

Part II: Determining the Meaning   Match the vocabulary words to their dictionary definitions.

___ 11. expedient
___ 12. ignominious
___ 13. recompensed
___ 14. circumspection
___ 15. countenance
___ 16. impeachment
___ 17. disapprobation
___ 18. extenuations
___ 19. alacrity
___ 20. insatiable

A. deserving shame or disgrace
B. the face; expression of a face
C. briskness; cheerful readiness
D. not able to be satisfied
E. conducive to a result; sometimes conducive to advantage as opposed to right
F. caution; heedfulness
G. paid; made compensation for
H. discredited or degraded
I. disapproval
J. partial excuses; serve to make less serious

Vocabulary - *Gulliver's Travels* - Part Two Chapters I - IV

Part I: Using Prior Knowledge and Contextual Clues

Below are the sentences in which the vocabulary words appear in the text. Read the sentence. Use any clues you can find in the sentence combined with your prior knowledge, and write what you think the underlined words mean on the lines provided.

1. Finding it was likely to overblow, we took in our sprit-sail, and stood by to hand the fore-sail; but making foul weather, we looked the guns were all fast, and handed the **mizen**.

___

2. The wife minced a bit of meat, then crumbled some bread on a **trencher**, and placed it before me.

___

3. These creatures were the size or a large **mastiff**, but infinitely more nimble and fierce.

___

4. I hope the gentle reader will excuse me for dwelling on these and the like particulars, which however insignificant they may appear to **grovelling** vulgar minds, yet will certainly help a philosopher to enlarge his thoughts and imagination and apply them to the benefit of public as well as private life. . .

___

5. My master, **pursuant** to the advice of his friend, carried me in a box the next market-day to the neighbouring town, and took along with him his little daughter my nurse upon a pillow behind him.

___

6. I was that day shown to twelve sets of company, and as often forced to go over again with the same **fopperies**, till I was half dead with weariness and vexation.

___

7. . . . and, as to the **ignominy** of being carried about for a monster, I considered myself to be a perfect stranger in the country.

___

Vocabulary - *Gulliver's Travels* - Part Two Chapters I - IV Continued

8. But, I confess, that after I had been a little too copious in talking of my own beloved country, of our trade, and wars by sea and land, of our **schisms** in religion, that he could not forbear taking me up in his right hand. . .

_____

9. The King's palace is no regular **edifice**, but an heap of buildings about seven miles round.

_____

10. But when he goes abroad on solemn days, he is attended for state by a militia guard of five hundred horse, which indeed I thought was the most splendid sight that could be ever beheld, till I saw part of his army in **battalia**, whereof I shall find another occasion to speak.

_____

Part II: Determining the Meaning   Match the vocabulary words to their dictionary definitions.

___ 21. mizzen   A. divisions into mutually opposed parties
___ 22. trencher   B. proceeding conformably
___ 23. mastiff   C. the sail on the mast nearest the stern of a three-masted vessel
___ 24. grovelling D. a flat piece of wood on which meat is carved and served
___ 25. pursuant   E. a building, especially one of large size or imposing appearance
___ 26. fopperies   F. an army in battle array or on the march;
___ 27. ignominy   G. a large dog of ancient breed
___ 28. schisms   H. manners, practices, dress, etc. of a foolish, pretentious person
___ 29. edifice   I. without dignity or aspirations
___ 30. battalia   J. dishonor, infamy

Vocabulary *Gulliver's Travels* Part Two Chapters V - VIII

Part I: Using Prior Knowledge and Contextual Clues

Below are the sentences in which the vocabulary words appear in the text. Read the sentence. Use any clues you can find in the sentence combined with your prior knowledge, and write what you think the underlined words mean on the lines provided.

1. I remember, before the dwarf left the Queen, he followed us one day into those gardens, and my nurse having set me down, he and I being close together, near some dwarf apple trees, I must needs show my wit by a silly **allusion** between him and the trees, which happens to hold in their language as it doth in ours.

_____

2, 3. Once a **kite** hovering over the garden made a swoop at me, and if I had not resolutely drawn my hanger, and run under a thick **espalier**, he would have certainly carried me away in his talons.

_____

_____

4. His Majesty in another audience was at pains to **recapitulate** the sum of all I had spoken.

_____

5. These were searched and sought out through the whole nation, ...among such of the priesthood as were most deservedly distinguished by the sanctity of their lives, and the depth of their **erudition**; . . .

_____

6. I have **perused** many of their books, especially those in history and morality.

_____

7, 8. He was strongly bent to get me a woman of my own size, by whom I might **propagate** the breed: but I think I should rather have died than undergone the disgrace of leaving a **posterity** to be kept in cages like tame canary birds. . .

_____

_____

Vocabulary *Gulliver's Travels* Part Two Chapters V - VIII Continued

9. And as truth always forceth its way into rational minds, so this honest worthy gentleman, who had some tincture of learning, and very good sense, was immediately convinced of my **candor** and veracity.

___

10. The Captain understood my **raillery** very well, and merrily replied with the old English proverb, that he doubted my eyes were bigger than my belly. . . .

___

Part II: Determining the Meaning   Match the vocabulary words to their dictionary definitions.

___ 31. allusion
___ 32. kite
___ 33. espalier
___ 34. recapitulation
___ 35. erudition
___ 36. perused
___ 37. propagate
___ 38. posterity
___ 39. candor
___ 40. raillery

A. read; scrutinized
B. sincerity; honesty; purity of character
C. an indirect reference, as by implication; casual mention
D. banter; good-humored ridicule
E. a predatory bird having a long, forked tail
F. descendants; succeeding generations
G. a trellis or framework on which trees or shrubs are trained to grow in a flattened form
H. to cause animals to multiply or breed
I. summarizing or repeating
J. learning; scholarship; knowledge

Vocabulary *Gulliver's Travels* Part Three Chapters I - V

Part I: Using Prior Knowledge and Contextual Clues

Below are the sentences in which the vocabulary words appear in the text. Read the sentence. Use any clues you can find in the sentence combined with your prior knowledge, and write what you think the underlined words mean on the lines provided.

1. his inflamed his rage; he repeated his threatenings, and turning to his companions, spoke with great **vehemence**, in the Japanese language.

_____

2. . . .when all on a sudden it (the sun) became obscured, as I thought, in a manner very different from what happens by the **interposition** of a cloud.

_____

3. I happened rightly to **conjecture** that these were sent for orders to some person in authority upon this occasion.

_____

4. Their heads were all reclined either to the right or the left; one of their eyes turned inward, and the other directly up to the **zenith**.

_____

5. On these **packthreads** the people strung their petitions, which mounted up directly like the scraps of paper fastened by school-boys at the end of the string that holds their kite.

_____

6. . . .the astronomers descend into a large dome, ... situated at the depth of a hundred yards beneath the upper surface of the **adamant.**

_____

7. The sum of his **discourse** was to this effect.

_____

Vocabulary *Gulliver's Travels*   Part Three Chapters I - V Continued

8. He had been eight years upon a project for extracting sun-beams out of cucumbers, which were to be put into vials **hermetically** sealed, and let out to warm the air in raw inclement summers.

___

9. There was an astronomer who had undertaken to place a sun-dial upon the great weathercock on the town-house, by adjusting the annual and **diurnal** motions of the earth and sun, so as to answer and coincide with all accidental turnings by the wind.

___

10. . . . and promised if ever I had the good fortune to return to my native country, that I would do him justice, as the sole inventor of this wonderful machine; the form and contrivance of which I desired leave to **delineate** upon paper.

___

Part II: Determining the Meaning   Match the vocabulary words to their dictionary definitions.

___ 41. vehemence   A. the act of putting between; intervention in behalf of a person
___ 42. interposition   B. to infer from inconclusive evidence
___ 43. conjecture   C. portray in words; describe; sketch or trace in outline
___ 44. zenith   D. characterized by violence of feeling or endeavor; passionate
___ 45 packthreads   E. pertaining to day; daily
___ 46. adamant   F. the highest point; the culmination
___ 47. discourse   G. closed so as to be air-tight
___ 48. hermetically   H. a strong thread or twine for sewing or tying up packages
___ 49. diurnal   I. an impenetrably hard substance; unyielding
___ 50. delineate   J. conversation; a formal discussion as a dissertation or sermon

Vocabulary *Gulliver's Travels* Part Three Chapters VI - XI

Part I: Using Prior Knowledge and Contextual Clues

Below are the sentences in which the vocabulary words appear in the text. Read the sentence. Use any clues you can find in the sentence combined with your prior knowledge, and write what you think the underlined words mean on the lines provided.

1. This illustrious person had very usefully employed his studies in finding out effectual remedies for all diseases and corruptions, to which the several kinds of public administration are subject by the vices or infirmities of those who govern, as well as by the **licentiousness** of those who are to obey.

_____

2. I heard a very warm debate between two professors, about the most **commodious** and effectual ways and means of raising money without grieving the subject.

_____

3. It is allowed, that senates and great councils are often troubled with **redundant**, ebullient, and other peccant humors.

_____

4. By his skill in **necromancy**, he hath a power of calling whom he pleaseth from the dead, and commanding their service for twenty-four hours, but no longer; . . .

_____

5. I was struck with a profound veneration at the sight of Brutus, and could easily discover the most **consummate** virtue, the greatest intrepidity and firmness of mind, the truest love of his country, and general benevolence for mankind in every lineament of his countenance.

_____

6. But as to counts, marquesses, dukes, earls, and the like, I was not so **scrupulous**.

_____

Vocabulary *Gulliver's Travels* Part Three Chapters VI - XI Continued

7. Who first brought the pox into a noble house, which hath lineally descended in **scrofulous** tumours to their posterity.

_____

8. Perjury, oppression, subornation, fraud, **panderism**, and the like infirmities, were amongst the most excusable arts they had to mention, and for these I gave, as it was reasonable, great allowance.

_____

9. Some of our sailors, whether out of treachery or **inadvertence**, had informed the pilots that I was a stranger.

_____

10. In talking they forget the common **appellation** of things, and the names of persons, even of those who are their nearest friends and relations.

_____

Part II: Determining the Meaning   Match the vocabulary words to their dictionary definitions.

____ 51. licentiousness   A. carefully conforming to the dictates of conscience
____ 52. commodious   B. complete or perfect; of the highest quality
____ 53. redundant   C. the act of naming; the act of appealing; a name, or title
____ 54. necromancy   D. unrestrained by law or morality; beyond proper limits
____ 55. consummate   E. catering to the baser passions of others
____ 56. scrupulous   F. a mistake or oversight
____ 57. scrofulous   G. convenient or satisfactory for the purpose; spacious, roomy
____ 58. panderism   H. needlessly repetitive
____ 59. inadvertence   I. swelling of lymphatic glands and inflammation of the joints
____ 60. appellation   J. the pretended art of divination through communication with the dead; magic; conjuration

Vocabulary *Gulliver's Travels* Part Four Chapters I - V

Part I: Using Prior Knowledge and Contextual Clues

Below are the sentences in which the vocabulary words appear in the text. Read the sentence. Use any clues you can find in the sentence combined with your prior knowledge, and write what you think the underlined words mean on the lines provided.

1. These rogues whom I had picked up **debauched** my other men.

___

2. Then he neighed three or four times, but in so different a **cadence,** that I almost began to think he was speaking to himself in some language of his own.

___

3. But this animal seeming to receive my civilities with **disdain** shook his head, and bent his brows, softly raising up his right forefoot to remove my hand.

___

4. Then the bay tried me with a second word, much harder to be pronounced; but reducing it to the English **orthography**, may be spelt thus, *Houyhnhnm*.

___

5. The master horse ordered a **sorrel** nag, one of his servants, to untie the largest of these animals, and take him into the yard.

___

6. It was at first a very **insipid** diet, though common enough in many parts of Europe, but grew tolerable by time;...

___

7. It put me to the pains of many **circumlocutions** to give my master a right idea of what I spoke; for their language doth not abound in variety of words, because their wants and passions are fewer than among us.

___

Vocabulary *Gulliver's Travels* Part Four Chapters I - V Continued

8. . . . I am confident that the frequent use of salt among us . . . was first introduced only as a **provocative** to drink.

___

9. Power, government, war, law, punishment, and a thousand other things had no terms wherein that language could express them, which made the difficulty almost **insuperable**.

___

10. It is a **maxim** among these lawyers, that whatever hath been done before may legally be done again.

___

Part II: Determining the Meaning   Match the vocabulary words to their dictionary definitions.

___ 61.	debauched	A.	an axiom; an expression of a general truth
___ 62.	cadence	B.	a stimulant
___ 63.	disdain	C.	a horse of reddish-brown color
___ 64.	orthography	D.	a feeling, attitude, or show of scornful superiority
___ 65.	sorrel	E.	insurmountable; not to be overcome
___ 66.	insipid	F.	beat of any rhythmical movement
___ 67.	circumlocutions	G.	to cause to forsake allegiance
___ 68.	provocative	H.	that part of grammar which treats of letters and spelling
___ 69.	insuperable	I.	without distinctive, interesting or attractive qualities; dull
___ 70.	maxim	J.	speaking in a round about way; use of many words for few

Vocabulary *Gulliver's Travels* Part Four Chapters VI - IX

Part I: Using Prior Knowledge and Contextual Clues

Below are the sentences in which the vocabulary words appear in the text. Read the sentence. Use any clues you can find in the sentence combined with your prior knowledge, and write what you think the underlined words mean on the lines provided.

1. My master was yet wholly at a loss to understand what motives could incite this race of lawyers to perplex, disquiet, and weary themselves, and engage in a **confederacy** of injustice.

2. One great excellency in this tribe is their skill at **prognostics**, wherein they seldom fail; their predictions in real diseases, when they rise to any degree of malignity, generally portending death, which is always in their power, when recovery is not; . . . .

3. . . . .he was sure I must have been born of some noble family, because I far exceeded in shape, colour, and cleanliness, all the Yahoos of his nation, although I seemed to fail in strength and agility, which must be **imputed** to my different way of living from those other brutes; . . .

4. But it was decreed by fortune, my perpetual enemy, that so great a **felicity** should not fall to my share.

5. My master continuing his discourse, said there was nothing that rendered the Yahoos more **odious** than their undistinguishing appetite to devour everything that came in their way . . .

6. But I could have easily **vindicated** human kind from the imputation of singularity upon the last article.

7. For, he only meant to observe what **parity** there was in our natures.

Vocabulary *Gulliver's Travels* Part Four Chapters VI - IX Continued

8. For now I could no longer deny that I was a real Yahoo in every limb and feature, since the females had a natural **propensity** to me, as one of their own species.

___

9. Every fourth year, at the **vernal** equinox, there is a representative council of the whole nation.

___

10. In poetry they must be allowed to excel all other mortals; wherein the justness of their similes, and the minuteness, as well as exactness of their descriptions, are indeed **inimitable**.

___

Part II: Determining the Meaning   Match the vocabulary words to their dictionary definitions.

___ 71. confederacy
___ 72. prognostics
___ 73. imputed
___ 74. felicity
___ 75. odious
___ 76. vindicated
___ 77. parity
___ 78. propensity
___ 79. vernal
___ 80. inimitable

A. pertaining to spring
B. attributed to; regarded as owing, as an effect to a cause
C. cannot be imitated or reproduced; matchless
D. a league or alliance; a conspiracy
E. hateful or detestable; obnoxious
F. forecasting what is to come; predictions
G. defended; set free; avenged; justified
H. equality
I. natural inclination or tendency
J. high degree of happiness; singular grace as of manner

Vocabulary *Gulliver's Travels* Part Four Chapters X - XII

Part I: Using Prior Knowledge and Contextual Clues

Below are the sentences in which the vocabulary words appear in the text. Read the sentence. Use any clues you can find in the sentence combined with your prior knowledge, and write what you think the underlined words mean on the lines provided.

1. . . . but I was infinitely delighted with the station of an humble **auditor** in such conversations, where nothing passed but what was useful, expressed in the fewest and most significant words . .

_____

2. I admired the strength, **comeliness** and speed of the inhabitants; . . .

_____

3. . . . for they alleged that because I had some **rudiments** of reason, added to the natural pravity of those animals, it was to be feared I might be able to seduce them into the woody and mountainous parts of the country, and bring them in troops by night to destroy the Houyhnhnms' cattle. . .

_____

4. . . . a decree of the general assembly in this country is expressed by the word *hnhloayn* which signifies an **exhortation**, as near as I can render it; for they have no conception how a rational creature can be compelled, but only advised or exhorted, because no person can disobey reason without giving up his claim to be a rational creature.

_____

5. I returned home, and consulting with the sorrel nag, we went into a **copse** at some distance, where I with my knife, and he with a sharp flint fastened very artificially after their manner to a wooden handle, cut down several oak wattels about the thickness of a walking-staff, and some larger pieces.

_____

6. But he added that since I professed so inviolable attachment to truth, I must give him my word of honour to bear him company in this voyage. . .

_____

Vocabulary *Gulliver's Travels* Part Four Chapters X - XII Continued

7. He **accoutered** me with other necessaries all new, which I aired for twenty-four hours before I would use them.

8. He said it was altogether impossible to find such a solitary island as I had desired to live in; but I might command in my own house, and pass my time in a manner as **recluse** as I pleased.

9. And it is highly probable that such travellers who shall hereafter visit the countries described in this work of mine, may, by detecting my errors (if there be any), and adding many new discoveries of their own, justle me out of **vogue**, and stand in my place, making the world forget that I was ever an author.

10. However, if those whom it more concerns think fit to be of another opinion, I am ready to **depose**, when I shall be lawfully called, that no European did ever visit these countries before me.

Part II: Determining the Meaning   Match the vocabulary words to their dictionary definitions.

___ 81. auditor   A. one who lives withdrawn from the world
___ 82. comeliness   B. the act of giving urgent advice or admonition as to conduct
___ 83. rudiments   C pleasing appearance; fair; handsome; proper
___ 84. exhortation   D give sworn testimony; to lay aside; remove from office
___ 85 copse   E. fashion at a particular time; current use
___ 86. inviolable   F. a hearer; one authorized to audit accounts
___ 87. accoutered   G. beginnings; first attempts; elementary
___ 88. recluse   H. a wood or thicket of small trees and bushes
___ 89. vogue   I. not to be violated; treated as if sacred
___ 90. depose   J. equipped with trappings; arrayed

ANSWER KEY VOCABULARY *Gulliver's Travels*

Part One Chapters I-IV	Part One Chapters V-VIII	Part Two Chapters I-IV	Part Two Chapters V-VIII
1. J	11. E	21. C	31. C
2. D	12. A	22. D	32. E
3. H	13. G	23. G	33. G
4. F	14. F	24. I	34. I
5. I	15. B	25. B	35. J
6. G	16. H	26. H	36. A
7. A	17. I	27. J	37. H
8. E	18. J	28. A	38. F
9. C	19. C	29. E	39. B
10. B	20. D	30. F	40. D

Part Three Chapters I-V	Part Three Chapters VI-XI	Part Four Chapters I-V	Part Four Chapters VI-IX
41. D	51. D	61. G	71. D
42. A	52. G	62. F	72. F
43. B	53. H	63. D	73. B
44. F	54. J	64. H	74. J
45. H	55. B	65. C	75. E
46. I	56. A	66. I	76. G
47. J	57. I	67. J	77. H
48. G	58. E	68. B	78. I
49. E	59. F	69. E	79. A
50. C	60. C	70. A	80. C

Part Four
Chapters X-XII
81. F
82. C
83. G
84. B
85. H
86. I
87. J
88. A
89. E
90. D

DAILY LESSONS

LESSON ONE *Gulliver's Travels*

Objectives
1. To introduce the *Gulliver's Travels* unit
2. To give students some background information about Swift, his times and his works
3. To take notes while watching a filmstrip/video
4. To explain and assign Writing Assignment 1

Activity #1
Do a group KWL Sheet with the students (form included.) Many students will have heard of *Gulliver's Travels*, and will have information to share. Put this information in the K column (what I know.) Ask students what they want to find out, and put it in the W column (what I want to find out.) Keep the sheet and refer back to it after reading the novel, and complete the L column (what I learned.) Students may also enjoy talking about trips they have made.

Activity #2
Show a film(strip)/video about Swift and his works, including *Gulliver's Travels*. You may want students to use the video note-taking form while they are watching it. The form is purposely generic, because there are many different films available.

Activity #3
Distribute the materials students will use in this unit. Explain in detail how students are to use these materials.

Study Guides Students should preview the study guide questions before each reading assignment to get a feeling for what events and ideas are important in that section. After reading the section, students will (as a class or individually) answer the questions to review the important events and ideas from that section of the book. Students should keep the study guides as study materials for the unit test.

Reading Assignment Sheet You need to fill in the reading assignment sheet to let students know when their reading has to be completed. You can either write the assignment sheet on a side blackboard or bulletin board and leave it there for students to see each day, or you can "ditto" copies for each student to have. In either case, you should advise students to become very familiar with the reading assignments so they know what is expected of them.

Extra Activities Center The resource sections of this unit contain suggestions for a library of related books and articles in your classroom as well as crossword and word search puzzles. Make an extra activities center in your room where you will keep these materials for students to use. (Bring the books and articles in from the library and keep several copies of the puzzles on hand.) Explain to students that these materials are available for students to use when they finish reading assignments or other class work early.

Nonfiction Assignment Sheet Explain to students that they each are to read at least one non-fiction piece from the in-class library at some time during the unit. Students will fill out a nonfiction assignment sheet after completing the reading to help you evaluate their reading experiences and to help the students think about and evaluate their own reading experiences.

Books Each school has its own rules and regulations regarding student use of school books. Advise students of the procedures that are normal for your school.

Activity #4
    Distribute Writing Assignment

KWL *Gulliver's Travels*

Directions: Before reading, think about what you already know about Jonathan Swift and/or Gulliver's Travels. Write the information in the K column. Think about what you would like to find out from reading the book. Write your questions in the W column. After you have read the book, use the L column to write the answers to your questions from the W column, and anything else you remember from the book.

K **What I Know**	**W** **What I Want to Find Out**	**L** **What I Learned**

LESSON ONE *Gulliver's Travels*

Filmstrip/Video Note-Taking Form *Gulliver's Travels*

Directions: Use this form to help yourself remember information from the film. Read the categories before watching the film. Then, while you are watching, record important information in the appropriate column. You may want to check with classmates after you are finished, and share your information.

About Jonathan Swift	About *Gulliver's Travels*	Other Information

WRITING ASSIGNMENT #1 *Gulliver's Travels*

Student's Name _____ Class _____

PROMPT

    Your assignment is to answer the question number _____ from the list entitled EXTRA WRITING ASSIGNMENTS/DISCUSSION QUESTIONS.

PREWRITING

    You are being given this assignment now so that as you read *Gulliver's Travels* you can pay particular attention to the parts which may help you answer your question.

    As you read the book, you will probably think "Oh, this part could have something to do with my question." When you come across examples or ideas like that, jot them down on a piece of paper -- whether it is a page reference in your book or an idea which pops into your head -- write it down. This will make the actual writing of the paper easier.

DRAFTING

    You should begin with an introductory paragraph giving your reader the topic of your paper. Change the question you are answering into a statement, and use this as an introduction. (Example: What effect did each of Gulliver's adventures have upon him? Gulliver had many adventures. Each had an effect upon him. In this paper I will explain the effects that each of his adventures had upon Gulliver.)

    The body of your composition should contain information related to your question. You may want to summarize a section of the book, or briefly retell an event. You may also use direct quotes from the novel. If you do this, use quotation marks around each quote, and make sure to cite each one at the end of the quote. (Example: Swift, page 112.)

    Write a paragraph in which you restate your topic and summarize your conclusions.

PROMPT

    When you finish the rough draft of your paper, ask a student who sits near you to read it. After reading your rough draft, he/she should tell you what he/she liked best about your work, which parts were difficult to understand, and ways in which your work could be improved. Reread your paper considering your critic's comments, and make the corrections you think are necessary.

PROOFREADING

    Do a final proofreading of your paper double-checking your grammar, spelling, organization, and the clarity of your ideas.

    After your paper is written, you will be asked to give a summary of your answer in order to lead a class discussion of the topic your question examines.

EXTRA WRITING ASSIGNMENTS AND/OR DISCUSSION QUESTIONS
Gulliver's Travels

<u>Interpretive</u>

1. What effect did each of Gulliver's adventures have upon him?

2. Gulliver is quite a changed man after all his travels, when he sits down to write this book. What effect do his experiences have upon the way he relates his travels?

3. Explain the phrase, "Beauty is in the eye of the beholder" as it relates to *Gulliver's Travels*.

4. What comments does Swift (not Gulliver) make about religion in *Gulliver's Travels*? Use specific examples from the text to support your answers.

5. What comments does Swift (not Gulliver) make about the nature of man in *Gulliver's Travels*? Use specific examples from the text to support your answers.

6. What comments does Swift (not Gulliver) make about education in *Gulliver's Travels*? Use specific examples from the text to support your answers.

7. Swift's views and Gulliver's views are often different. Explain how Swift uses Gulliver to make his points to us.

8. In Book One, Chapter II, Gulliver says that he thinks it necessary to "justify [his] character in point of cleanliness to the world." Explain why he feels this need and attempts to do so throughout the books.

9. What are the conflicts in *Gulliver's Travels* and how are they resolved?

10. Explain Swift's (not Gulliver's) views on science. Use specific examples from the text to support your answers.

<u>Critical</u>

11. Compare Gulliver's treatment of the Lilliputians with the Brobdingnagians' treatment of Gulliver.

12. Compare and contrast the governments of the lands Gulliver visited, and explain Swift's (not Gulliver's) comment on the subject of government.

13. Compare and contrast views on war in each of the lands Gulliver visited, and explain Swift's (not Gulliver's) comment on the subject of war.

Gulliver Extra Discussion Questions page 2

14. Gulliver is consumed with concern about what others think of him and his native countrymen. Give examples of this concern and explain its effect on his actions and on the themes of the book.

15. Explain the use of vice vs. virtue in *Gulliver's Travels*.

16. What is a tragedy? Is *Gulliver's Travels* a tragedy in the literary sense of the word? Explain why or why not.

17. Explain how *Gulliver's Travels* is a book about rational vs. irrational, and note the conclusions Swift would have us draw from his work.

18. Explain the devices Swift uses to make us willingly suspend our disbelief of these unusual adventures.

19. What is satire? Explain how Swift uses it in *Gulliver's Travels*, and explain its effect on us, the readers.

20. Swift makes many comments about the nature or man, education, religion, etc. Choose three of these comments. Do you agree or disagree with Swift? Support your answers, using passages from the text as well as outside sources such as the newspaper or magazine articles.

21. What is irony? Give specific examples of Swift's use of irony in *Gulliver's Travels* and explain the effect of the use of irony on us, the readers.

22. Considering all of Gulliver's travels, explain what Swift would consider an ideal race of beings, and explain why or why not man is or could become that race.

23. Considering *Gulliver's Travels*, define "man" as you think Swift would. Use examples from the text to support your answers when possible.

24. What one theme unites all the four books of *Gulliver's Travels*? Support your answer with specific examples from the text.

Gulliver Extra Discussion Questions page 3

Personal Opinion

25. Could anything be gained by adding a Book Five to *Gulliver's Travels*? Explain why or why not in relation to the themes and structure of the book.

26. What is the value of reading *Gulliver's Travels* today? What can the modern-day reader gain from reading it?

LESSON TWO *Gulliver's Travels*

Objectives
1. To do the prereading work for Book One Chapters I-IV
2. To begin reading *Gulliver's Travels*
3. To give students the opportunity to practice their oral reading skills
4. To give the teacher an opportunity to evaluate students' reading abilities
5. To assign and discuss the Non-Fiction Assignment Sheet.

Activity #1

Have students complete the prereading work for Book One Chapters I-IV of *Gulliver's Travels*. They should review the study questions and do the required vocabulary work.

Activity #2

Read the first several pages of the book aloud to the class to model correct oral reading techniques. Have students begin reading *Gulliver's Travels* orally. You probably know the best way to get readers within your class; pick students at random, ask for volunteers, or use whatever method works best for your group. If you have not yet completed an oral reading evaluation for your students this marking period, this would be a good opportunity to do so. A form is included with this unit for your convenience.

If you have not given students a grade for oral reading this quarter, you may want to do so during this unit. If so, there is an oral reading evaluation form included for your convenience.

Activity #3

Distribute copies of the Nonfiction Assignment Sheet. Review and discuss it with students.

NONFICTION ASSIGNMENT SHEET *GULLIVER'S TRAVELS*
(To be completed after reading the required nonfiction article)

Name _____ Date _____ Class _____

Title of Nonfiction Read _____

Written By _____ Publication Date _____

I. Factual Summary: Write a short summary of the piece you read.

II. Vocabulary:
    1. With which vocabulary words in the piece did you encounter some degree of difficulty?

    2. How did you resolve your lack of understanding with these words?

III. Interpretation: What was the main point the author wanted you to get from reading his work?

IV. Criticism:
    1. With which points of the piece did you agree or find easy to accept? Why?

    2. With which points of the piece did you disagree or find difficult to believe? Why?

V. Personal Response: What do you think about this piece? OR How does this piece influence your ideas?

ORAL READING EVALUATION *Gulliver's Travels*

Name_____Class_____Date _____

SKILL	EXCELLENT	GOOD	AVERAGE	FAIR	POOR
Fluency	5	4	3	2	1
Clarity	5	4	3	2	1
Audibility	5	4	3	2	1
Pronunciation	5	4	3	2	1
_____	5	4	3	2	1
_____	5	4	3	2	1

Total _____ Grade _____

Comments:

LESSON THREE *Gulliver's Travels*

Objectives:
1. To review the main ideas and events from Book One Chapters I-IV
2. To practice rereading to locate specific information

Activity #1

Give students a few minutes to formulate answers for the study guide questions for Book One, Chapters I-IV. Write the answers on the board or overhead transparency so students can have the correct answers for study purposes. Note: It is a good practice in public speaking and leadership skills for individual students to take charge of leading the discussions of the study questions. Perhaps a different student could go to the front of the class and lead the discussion each day that the study questions are discussed during this unit. Of course, the teacher should guide the discussion when appropriate and be sure to fill in any gaps the students leave.

Activity #2

If necessary, demonstrate how to reread to locate information in the text. Suggest to the students that they indicate the page number where they found each answer on their study question sheet or in their notebook. If students own the books, you may want to show them how to highlight specific information and make margin notes.

LESSON FOUR *Gulliver's Travels*

Objectives:
1. To do the pre-reading work for Book One Chapters V-VIII
2. To read Book One Chapters V-VIII
3. To give students the opportunity to practice their oral reading skills
4. To give students the opportunity to practice their listening skills
5. To review the main events from Book One

Activity #1

Have students review the study questions and do the required vocabulary work.

Activity #2

Tell students they will be reading aloud in pairs. One partner will listen and follow along in their book while the other reads aloud. They should switch off frequently. Assign partners, or allow students to choose their partners. Depending on your room arrangement, you may want to allow students to move their desks around, or to sit in various locations around the room. Have students read Book One Chapters V-VIII.

Activity #3

Have students continue working in pairs. Assign each pair of students a few study guide questions to answer. Have each pair present their answers aloud for the class.

LESSON FIVE *Gulliver's Travels*

Objectives:
1. To do the pre-reading work for Book Two Chapters I-IV
2. To read Book Two Chapters I-IV silently
3. To review the main ideas and events of Book Two Chapters I-IV

Activity #1

Have students review the study questions and do the required vocabulary work.

Activity #2.

Have students read Book Two Chapters I-IV silently.

Activity #3

Have students answer the study questions individually, and then check their answers with a classmate.

LESSON SIX *Gulliver's Travels*

Objectives
1. To do the pre-reading work for Book Two Chapters V-VIII
2. To read Book Two Chapters V-VIII silently
3. To review the main events and ideas of Book Two

Activity #1

Have students review the study questions and do the required vocabulary work.

Activity #2.

Have students read Book Two Chapters V-VIII silently.

Activity #3

Use the multiple choice format of the story questions for a quiz on Book Two. If time permits, discuss the answers after you have collected the papers.

LESSON SEVEN *Gulliver's Travels*

Objective:
    To give students the opportunity to practice their writing skills

Activity #1
    Distribute Writing Assignment #2 and discuss the directions in detail. Allow students ample time to complete the assignment. Collect the papers at the end of the period. If time permits, students may wish to share their papers with each other. You may also want to display them on a bulletin board.

    A Writing Evaluation Form is provided for your use in evaluating your students' writing.

WRITING ASSIGNMENT #2 *Gulliver's Travels*

PROMPT

Gulliver has written four books about his travels. Your assignment is to make a travelogue. A travelogue is a journal that describes your trip. If you have been on a vacation, tell all about that. If you haven't ever been on a trip or don't want to tell about a vacation you have had, write about a vacation trip you think you would like to take.

The point of the assignment is for you to practice writing vividly, describing the trip so the reader will enjoy it. Your travelogue should be 500 - 750 words long. You may use photos, magazine pictures, or drawings.

PREWRITING

Make a list of places you have been, or places you would like to go. Select one to write about. Make another list of everything you know about that place. Be sure to include adjectives that describe the place and adjectives to describe your feelings about the place. If you are writing about a place you have been, add details about when you went there, and with whom you traveled. Think about whether or not the trip changed you, and how.

You need to make a few basic decisions: Are you going to have any drawings or pictures with your travelogue? Where will they go? How long will you make the travelogue? Once you have made these decisions, write a rough draft of your travelogue.

DRAFTING

In your introductory paragraph, tell who you are and where you went on your journey. You may also tell why you went there. In the body of the travelogue, describe in detail the things you saw and the people you met. Also include your feelings and reactions about your journey. You should have a concluding paragraph that restates where you went, and summarizes your feelings about the trip.

PROMPT

After you have finished a rough draft of your travelogue, revise it yourself until you are happy with your work. Then, ask a student who sits near you to read your work and tell you what he/she likes best about it, and what things could be improved. Take another look at your travelogue, keeping in mind your critic's suggestions, and make the revisions you feel are necessary.

PROOFREADING

Do a final proofreading of your paper, double checking your grammar, spelling, organization and the clarity of your ideas.

WRITING EVALUATION FORM *Gulliver's Travels*

Name _____ Date _____ Class _____

Writing Assignment #___ for *Gulliver's Travels*

Circle One For Each Item:

Introduction	excellent	good	fair	poor
Body Paragraphs	excellent	good	fair	poor
Summary	excellent	good	fair	poor
Grammar	excellent	good	fair	poor (errors noted)
Spelling	excellent	good	fair	poor (errors noted)
Punctuation	excellent	good	fair	poor (errors noted)
Legibility	excellent	good	fair	poor (errors noted)

Strengths:

Weaknesses:

Comments/Suggestions:

LESSON EIGHT *Gulliver's Travels*

Objectives
1. To read Book Three, Chapters I-V
2. To review the main events and ideas of Book Three, Chapters I-V
3. To give students the opportunity to read silently

Activity #1
　　Have students preview the study questions and do the vocabulary work for Book Three, Chapters I-V.

Activity #2
　　Have students read Book Three, Chapters I-V silently.

Activity #3
　　Do the study guide for Book Three, Chapters I-V together. Ask the questions and let the students answer. Allow time for any necessary discussion. Write the correct answers to the questions on the board or overhead projector so students can copy them down for study use.

LESSON NINE *Gulliver's Travels*

Objectives
1. To read Book Three, Chapters VI-XI
2. To review the main events and ideas of Book Three, Chapters VI-XI
3. To give students the opportunity to practice reading silently

Activity #1
　　Have students preview the study questions and do the vocabulary work for Book Three, Chapters VI-XI. You may want to allow students to work with a partner on this activity.

Activity #2
　　Have students read Book Three, Chapters VI-XI silently.

Activity #3
　　You may want to have students write their answers to the short answer study questions while they are reading. You could use this for an open-book quiz grade.

LESSON TEN Gulliver's Travels

Objectives:
1. To read Book Four, Chapters I-V
2. To give students the opportunity to practice reading silently
3. To give students the opportunity to practice reading orally
4. To review the main events and ideas from Book Four, Chapters I-V

Activity #1

Have students preview the study questions and do the vocabulary work for Book Four, Chapters I-V.

Activity #2

Depending on the needs and abilities of your group, have students read either silently or orally.

Activity #3

Have students answer the study guide questions independently. Then have them exchange papers for correcting. You may want to use this as a quiz grade.

LESSON ELEVEN *Gulliver's Travels*

Objectives:
1. To read Book Four, Chapters VI-IX
2. To give the students the opportunity to read silently
3. To discuss the main events and ideas of Book Four, Chapters VI-IX

Activity #1

Have students preview the study questions and do the vocabulary work for Book Four, Chapters I-V.

Activity #2

Have students read the selection silently. You may want to allow them to write the answers to the study guide questions as they find them in the text.

Activity #3

Have each student write three questions about the reading. Students can trade papers and answer each other's questions, or you can use them as a whole-class review.

LESSON TWELVE *Gulliver's Travels*

Objectives:
1. To read Book Four, Chapters X-XII
2. To give students the opportunity to practice reading orally
3. To discuss the main events and ideas of Book Four.

Activity #1

Have students preview the study questions and do the vocabulary work for Book Four, Chapters X-XII

Activity #2

Have students read Book Four, Chapters X-XII orally.

Activity #3

Distribute copies of the multiple choice questions for Book Four, and have students answer them. You may want to use this as a quiz grade.

LESSON THIRTEEN *Gulliver's Travels*

Objectives
1. To have students look in more depth at *Gulliver's Travels*
2. To give students the opportunity to practice their writing skills
3. To give the teacher the opportunity to evaluate students' writing skills

Activity #1

Give students this class period to work on Writing Assignment #1. If more than one student is working on the same question, you may want to let them conference quietly.

If students are having difficulty with the assignment, you may want to model a response for the group.

Activity #2

Hold brief individual conferences with students about their writing assignment. Allow students a few days to revise their papers. I suggest grading the revisions on an A-C-E scale (all revisions well done, some revisions made, or no revisions made.) This will speed your grading time and still give some credit for the students' efforts.

Assign the due date for the assignment.

LESSONS FOURTEEN and FIFTEEN *Gulliver's Travels*

Objective:
>To study in more detail the characters Gulliver met in his travels

Activity #1
>Divide your class into ten groups, one for each of the following:

>1. Lilliputians
>2. Blefuscuians
>3. Brobdingnagians
>4. Laputians
>5. Lagadians
>6. Glubbdubdribians
>7. Luggnaggians
>8. Houyhnhnms
>9. Yahoos
>10. English/Europeans

Each group should write down the characteristics of the "people" they are assigned and Gulliver's reaction them. In other words, for example, what were the main characteristics of the Lilliputians, and what did Gulliver think of them?, etc.

Activity #2
>Have a spokesperson from each group report the group's findings from the group activity in Lesson Fourteen. Use these reports as a springboard for discussing each of the groups of characters in Gulliver's Travels.

>You may want to have a large piece of chart paper on the chalkboard or bulletin board. Put the name of each of the groups at the top of the chart. Have a writer from each group record the characteristics of the group. Students with artistic ability could draw their interpretations of what the characters look like.

LESSON SIXTEEN *Gulliver's Travels*

Objective

To discuss *Gulliver's Travels* on a deeper than "direct recall" level

Activity

Discuss the extra questions provided with this packet by having students read or summarize their Writing Assignment #1 papers. Each student should give an answer to the question he worked on for his paper. Use these "reports" as a springboard for discussion of each question.

Write the "answers" to the questions on the board (or overhead projector transparency) for students to copy for study use. (Or you could just allow students to take notes and then show a transparency at the end of the discussions as a brief review so students can check their notes.)

Collect each student's writing assignment after he finishes his oral presentation.

NOTE: Depending on the depth of your discussions, you may need to insert an extra day or two of discussions here to complete all the questions you assigned. There is no way I can predict the number of class periods you will need; it depends on class size, number of interruptions, depth of discussion, etc.

LESSON SEVENTEEN *Gulliver's Travels*

Objectives:
1. To widen the breadth of students' knowledge about the topics discussed or touched upon in *Gulliver's Travels*.
2. To check students' non-fiction assignments.

Activity

Ask each student to give a brief oral report about the nonfiction work he/she read for the nonfiction assignment. Your criteria for evaluating this report will vary depending on the level of your students. You may wish for students to give a complete report without using notes of any kind, or you may want students to read directly from a written report, or you may want to do something in between these two extremes. Just make students aware of your criteria in ample time for them to prepare their reports.

Start with one student's report, After that, ask if anyone else in the class has read on a topic related to the first student's report. If no one has, choose another student at random. After each report, be sure to ask if anyone has a report related to the one just completed. That will help keep a continuity during the discussion of the reports.

LESSON EIGHTEEN *Gulliver's Travels*

Objective:
   To write a persuasive letter

Activity #1
   Ask students if they have ever been persuaded to do something. Discuss the methods the persuader used. Read a few examples of persuasive writing aloud to the students. discuss the ways that persuasive writing differs from other types of writing. Make a list of words or phrases that are often used in persuasive writing, and post it somewhere in the room.

Activity #2
   Distribute copies of Writing Assignment #3. Allow students to work on the assignment for the remainder of the class time. Set a due date for the assignment.

WRITING ASSIGNMENT #3 *Gulliver's Travels*

PROMPT
When Gulliver returned from his journey to the Houyhnhnms, he could no longer bear the sight or company of human beings(Yahoos). Write a letter to Gulliver and persuade him to once again keep company with his countrymen., especially his wife and family.

PREWRITING
Look through the story to find examples of the way Gulliver acted before he went to the land of the Houyhnhnms. Observe people acting "like people" and record your observations.

DRAFTING
Begin with an introductory paragraph. Tell Gulliver who you are, and why you are writing.

In the body of your letter, remind Gulliver of the way he felt about humans before his journey to the country of the Houyhnhnms. You may want to give examples from the text showing his civilized, human behavior. Write a paragraph showing the good qualities of his wife and family and humans in general. Give specific examples, based on your prewriting observations. Finally, offer a paragraph of suggestions for helping Gulliver return to the company of humans.

End your letter with a concluding paragraph in which you give Gulliver encouragement for returning to human company, and thank him for reading your letter.

PROMPT
When you finish the rough draft of your paper, ask a student who sits near you to read it. After reading your rough draft, he/she should tell you what he/she liked best about your work, which parts were difficult to understand, and ways in which your work could be improved. Reread your paper considering your critic's comments, and make the corrections you think are necessary.

PROOFREADING
Do a final proofreading of your paper double-checking your grammar, spelling, organization, and the clarity of your ideas.

LESSON NINETEEN *Gulliver's Travels*

Objectives
To review the main ideas presented in *Gulliver's Travels*

Activity #1
Choose one of the review games/activities included in the packet and spend your class period as outlined there.

Activity #2
Remind students of the date for the Unit Test. Stress the review of the Study Guides and their class notes as a last minute, brush-up review for homework.

REVIEW GAMES / ACTIVITIES

1. Ask the class to make up a unit test for *Gulliver's Travels*. The test should have 4 sections: multiple choice, true/false, short answer and essay. Students may use 1/2 period to make the test, including a separate answer sheet, and then swap papers and use the other 1/2 class period to take a test a classmate has devised. (open book)

2. Take 1/2 period for students to make up true and false questions (including the answers). Collect the papers and divide the class into two teams. Draw a big tic-tac-toe board on the chalk board. Make one team X and one team O. Ask questions to each side, giving each student one turn. If the question is answered correctly, that student's team's letter (X or O) is placed in the box. If the answer is incorrect, no mark is placed in the box. The object is to get three marks in a row like tic-tac-toe. You may want to keep track of the number of games won for each team.

3. Take 1/2 period for students to make up questions (true/false and short answer). Collect the questions. Divide the class into two teams. You'll alternate asking questions to individual members of teams A & B (like in a spelling bee). The question keeps going from A to B until it is correctly answered, then a new question is asked. A correct answer does not allow the team to get another question. Correct answers are +2 points; incorrect answers are -1 point.

4. Allow students time to quiz each other (in pairs) from their study guides and class notes.

5. Give students a *Gulliver's Travels* crossword puzzle to complete.

6. Divide your class into two teams. Use the *Gulliver's Travels* crossword words with their letters jumbled as a word list. Student 1 from Team A faces off against Student 1 from Team B. You write the first jumbled word on the board. The first student (1A or 1B) to unscramble the word wins the chance for his/her team to score points. If 1A wins the jumble, go to student 2A and give him/her a clue. He/she must give you the correct word which matches that clue. If he/she does, Team A scores a point, and you give student 3A a clue for which you expect another correct response. Continue giving Team A clues until some team member makes an incorrect response. An incorrect response sends the game back to the jumbled-word face off, this time with students 2A and 2B. Instead of repeating giving clues to the first few students of each team, continue with the student after the one who gave the last incorrect response on the team.

LESSON TWENTY *Gulliver's Travels*

Objective
    To review all of the vocabulary work done in this unit

Activity
    Choose one (or more) of the vocabulary review activities listed on the next page(s) and spend your class period as directed in the activity. Some of the materials for these review activities are located in the Vocabulary Resources section of this unit.

VOCABULARY REVIEW ACTIVITIES

1. Divide your class into two teams and have an old-fashioned spelling or definition bee.

2. Give each of your students (or students in groups of two, three or four) a *Gulliver's Travels* Vocabulary Word Search Puzzle. The person (group) to find all of the vocabulary words in the puzzle first wins.

3. Give students a *Gulliver's Travels* Vocabulary Word Search Puzzle without the word list. The person or group to find the most vocabulary words in the puzzle wins.

4. Use a *Gulliver's Travels* Vocabulary Crossword Puzzle. Put the puzzle onto a transparency on the overhead projector (so everyone can see it), and do the puzzle together as a class.

5. Give students a *Gulliver's Travels* Vocabulary Matching Worksheet to do.

6. Divide your class into two teams. Use the *Gulliver's Travels* vocabulary words with their letters jumbled as a word list. Student 1 from Team A faces off against Student 1 from Team B. You write the first jumbled word on the board. The first student (1A or 1B) to unscramble the word wins the chance for his/her team to score points. If 1A wins the jumble, go to student 2A and give him/her a definition. He/she must give you the correct spelling of the vocabulary word which fits that definition. If he/she does, Team A scores a point, and you give student 3A a definition for which you expect a correctly spelled matching vocabulary word. Continue giving Team A definitions until some team member makes an incorrect response. An incorrect response sends the game back to the jumbled-word face off, this time with students 2A and 2B. Instead of repeating giving definitions to the first few students of each team, continue with the student after the one who gave the last incorrect response on the team. For example, if Team B wins the jumbled-word face-off, and student 5B gave the last incorrect answer for Team B, you would start this round of definition questions with student 6B, and so on. The team with the most points wins!

7. Have students write a story in which they correctly use as many vocabulary words as possible. Have students read their compositions orally. Post the most original compositions on your bulletin board!

LESSON TWENTY-ONE *Gulliver's Travels*

Objective
To review the main ideas presented in *Gulliver's Travels*

Activity #1
Use any of the review activities from Lessons Sixteen or Seventeen that you did not already use.

Activity #2
Take on the persona of "The Answer Person." Allow students to ask any question about the book. Answer the questions, or tell students where to look in the book to find the answer.

Activity #3
Students may enjoy playing charades with events from the story. Select a student to start. Give him/her a card with a scene or event from the story. Allow the players to use their books to find the scene being described. The first person to guess each charade performs the next one.

Activity #4
Play a categories-type quiz game. Make an overhead transparency of the categories form. Divide the class into teams of three or four players each. Have each team choose a recorder and a banker. choose a team to go first. That team will choose a category and point amount. Ask the question to the entire class.(Use the Study Guide Quiz and Vocabulary questions.) Give the teams one minute to discuss the answer and write it down. Walk around the room and check the answers. Each team that answers correctly receives the points. (Incorrect answers are not penalized; they just don't receive any points.) Cross out that square on the playing board. Play continues until all squares have been used. The winning team is the one with the most points. You can assign bonus points to any square or squares you choose.

NOTE: If students do not need the extra review, omit this lesson and go on to the test.

QUIZ GAME *Gulliver's Travels*

Vocabulary	Lilliput	Brobdingnag	Laputa, etc.	Houyhnhnms
100	100	100	100	100
200	200	200	200	200
300	300	300	300	300
400	400	400	400	400
500	500	500	500	500

LESSON TWENTY-TWO *Gulliver's Travels*

Objective

To test the students' understanding of the main ideas and themes in Gulliver's Travels.

Activity #1

Distribute the *Gulliver's Travels* Unit Tests. Go over the instructions in detail and allow the students the entire class period to complete the exam.

Activity #2

Collect all test papers and assigned books prior to the end of the class period.

NOTES ABOUT THE UNIT TESTS IN THIS UNIT:

There are 5 different unit tests which follow.

There are two short answer tests which are based primarily on facts from the novel. The answer key short answer unit test 1 follows the student test. The answer key for short answer test 2 follows the student short answer unit test 2.

There is one advanced short answer unit test. It is based on the extra discussion questions and quotations. Use the matching key for short answer unit test 2 to check the matching section of the advanced short answer unit test. There is no key for the short answer questions and quotations. The answers will be based on the discussions you have had during class.

There are two multiple choice unit tests. Following the two unit tests, you will find an answer sheet on which students should mark their answers. The same answer sheet should be used for both tests; however, students' answers will be different for each test. Following the students' answer sheet for the multiple choice tests you will find your answer keys.

The short answer tests have a vocabulary section. You should choose 10 of the vocabulary words from this unit, read them orally and have the students write them down. Then, either have students write a definition or use the words in sentences.

UNIT TESTS

UNIT TEST 1 *Gulliver's Travels*

I. Matching

1. _____ Struldbrugs
2. _____ Glubbdubdrib
3. _____ Laputa
4. _____ Lilliput
5. _____ Flappers
6. _____ Glumdalclitch
7. _____ Yahoo
8. _____ Munodi
9. _____ Grildrig
10. _____ Lagado
11. _____ Blefuscu
12. _____ Luggnagg
13. _____ Flimnap
14. _____ Houyhnhnm
15. _____ Brobdingnag

A. Gulliver's name in Brobdingnag
B. Land of big people
C. Reasoning animals
D. Gulliver's enemy in Lilliput
E. Bestial man-like creature
F. People who live forever
G. Land of enemies of Lilliputians
H. Floating island
I. Governor here called forth dead persons
J. Gulliver licked the floor to the king here
K. Servants who hit their masters
L. Gulliver's friend in Lagado
M. Food Gulliver ate with Houyhnhnms
N. Word meaning "drink and be merry"
O. Land with the Academy of Projectors
P. Gulliver's "nurse" friend
Q. Land of little people

II. Short Answer

1. For what purpose did the Lilliputians learn rope dancing and "leaping and creeping"?

2. What were five of Gulliver's nine conditions of freedom in Lilliput?

3. About what were the Lilliputians fighting with the people across the water?

Gulliver Short Answer Unit Test 1 page 2

4. How did Gulliver end up living with the king and queen in Brobdingnag?

5. How did Gulliver attempt to please the king and queen in Brobdingnag -- and why did he do it?

6. Why didn't Gulliver's clothes fit in Laputa?

7. What was the purpose of the Academy of Projectors? What was the problem with the Academy?

8. Why did Gulliver conceal the secret of his dress from the Houyhnhnms?

9. Gulliver said he could "better endure the sight of a common Yahoo than of my own person." Why could he?

10. What did Gulliver conclude is the worst vice of mankind?

Gulliver Short Answer Unit Test 1 page 3

III. Essay

Answer with a complete paragraph:

Explain the phrase "beauty is in the eye of the beholder" as it relates to *Gulliver's Travels*.

Gulliver Short Answer Unit Test 1 page 4

IV. Vocabulary

Listen to the vocabulary words and spell them. After you have spelled all the words, go back and write down the definitions.

ANSWER KEY UNIT TEST 1 *Gulliver's Travels*

I. Matching

1. __F.__ Struldbrugs
2. __I.__ Glubbdubdrib
3. __H.__ Laputa
4. __Q.__ Lilliput
5. __K.__ Flappers
6. __P.__ Glumdalclitch
7. __E.__ Yahoo
8. __L.__ Munodi
9. __A.__ Grildrig
10. __O.__ Lagado
11. __G.__ Blefuscu
12. __J.__ Luggnagg
13. __D.__ Flimnap
14. __C.__ Houyhnhnms
15. __B.__ Brobdingnag

A. Gulliver's name in Brobdingnag
B. Land of big people
C. Reasoning animals
D. Gulliver's enemy in Lilliput
E. Bestial man-like creature
F. People who live forever
G. Land of enemies of Lilliputians
H. Floating island
I. Governor here called forth dead persons
J. Gulliver licked the floor to the king here
K. Servants who hit their masters
L. Gulliver's friend in Lagado
M. Food Gulliver ate with Houyhnhnms
N. Word meaning "drink and be merry"
O. Land with the Academy of Projectors
P. Gulliver's "nurse" friend
Q. Land of little people

II. Short Answer

1. For what purpose did the Lilliputians learn rope dancing and "leaping and creeping"?

    By the performance of these acts, they attempt to impress the Emperor, to gain political offices.

2. What were five of Gulliver's nine conditions of freedom in Lilliput?
    1. Gulliver won't leave without permission.
    2. He won't go into the city without permission and two hours warning to the citizens.
    3. Walk only on high road - not in meadows or fields.
    4. Won't step on anyone or anything and won't pick up people without their permission.
    5. Will carry messenger for Emperor once a month if necessary.
    6. Will be ally of Lilliput against Blefuscuian.
    7. Will help with construction and physical labor.
    8. Will survey circumference of Lilliput.
    9. For obedience to above, Gulliver will be fed as much food as 1728 Lilliputians would eat.

3. About what were the Lilliputians fighting with the people across the water?

Blefuscuians break their eggs on the big end, as was the religious custom until the present Lilliputian Emperor's grandfather decreed eggs should be broken on the small end. Big-Endings (who fled to Blefuscu) and Little-Endians (Lilliputians) have been fighting over which end of the egg to break first.

4. How did Gulliver end up living with the king and queen in Brobdingnag?

The farmer who found Gulliver took him from town to town, showing him to people for profit. He was summoned to bring Gulliver for the Queen's entertainment. The Queen liked the performance, and Gulliver interested her, so she bought him from the farmer, who willingly sold him (since he thought Gulliver would die soon anyway).

5. How did Gulliver attempt to please the king and queen in Brobdingnag -- and why did he do it?

He made cane chairs and a purse from the Queen's hair and he learned to play a tune on the spinet. He did it to try to restore his pride, so they would think better of him.

6. Why didn't Gulliver's clothes fit in Laputa?

The tailor calculated his height and then using mathematics calculated the appropriate size of his clothes (instead of taking many measurements). The tailor had made an error in his calculations.

7. What was the purpose of the Academy of Projectors? What was the problem with the Academy?

People who had visited the floating island learned a little about math and science and became dissatisfied with life on the ground when they returned. They began the Academy as a way of "putting arts, sciences, languages, and mechanics on a new foot." In the Academy, professors thought of new ways of doing things. The problem is that the ideas which are developed there are impractical and useless -- and don't work.

8. Why did Gulliver conceal the secret of his dress from the Houyhnhnms?

He realized that without his clothes, he looked much more like a Yahoo, the creatures he detested.

9. Gulliver said he could "better endure the sight of a common Yahoo than of my own person." Why could he?

Yahoos had vices, but men also had reason which they inappropriately used to increase their natural vices. He was ashamed to be a man.

10. What did Gulliver conclude is the worst vice of mankind?

Gulliver concluded that pride is the worst vice of mankind.

III. Essay: Grade the compositions on your own criteria

IV. Vocabulary: Choose ten of the vocabulary words to read orally to your class.

UNIT TEST 2 *Gulliver's Travels*

I. Matching

1. _____ Grildrig
2. _____ Lagado
3. _____ Flappers
4. _____ Glumdalclitch
5. _____ Glubbdubdrib
6. _____ Flimnap
7. _____ Yahoo
8. _____ Struldbrugs
9. _____ Lilliput
10. _____ Brobdingnag
11. _____ Luggnagg
12. _____ Munodi
13. _____ Laputa
14. _____ Houyhnhnms
15. _____ Blefuscu

A. Food Gulliver ate with Houyhnhnms
B. Gulliver's name in Brobdingnag
C. Reasoning animals
D. Governor here called forth dead persons
E. Land of enemies of Lilliputians
F. Bestial man-like creature
G. Land with the Academy of Projectors
H. Gulliver licked the king's floor here
I. Word meaning "drink and be merry"
J. Floating island
K. Land of big people
L. Gulliver's "nurse" friend
M. People who live forever
N. Gulliver's friend in Lagado
O. Gulliver's enemy in Lilliput
P. Servants who hit their masters
Q. Land of little people

II. Short Answer

1. How did Gulliver help the Lilliputians against the Blefuscuians?

2. The emperor of Lilliput wanted Gulliver to do more to help him finally crush the Blefuscuians so he could be emperor of all the lands. What was Gulliver's response?

3. Describe the people of Brobdingnag.

4. What was the King of Brobdingnag's reaction to Gulliver's accounts of English manners, laws, religion, and government?

Gulliver Short Answer Unit Test 2 page 2

5. What gift did Gulliver wish to give the King of Brobdingnag, and what was the King's reaction to the offer?

6. How did Gulliver describe the Laputians?

7. What were four of the projects Gulliver saw Professors attempting at the Academy of Projectors?

8. How did most of the other residents of Luggnagg feel about the Struldbrugs?

9. What human concept was almost never heard of in the land of the Houyhnhnms?

10. What effect did Gulliver's time with the Houyhnhnms have upon his view of his countrymen?

Gulliver Short Answer Unit Test 2 page 3

III. Essay

What effect did each of Gulliver's adventures have upon him?

Gulliver Short Answer Unit Test 1 page 4

IV. Vocabulary

    Listen to the vocabulary words and spell them. After you have spelled all the words, go back and write down the definitions.

ANSWER KEY   UNIT TEST 2 *Gulliver's Travels*

I. Matching

1. B. Grildrig
2. G. Lagado
3. P. Flappers
4. L. Glumdalclitch
5. D. Glubbdubdrib
6. O. Flimnap
7. F. Yahoo
8. M. Struldbrugs
9. Q. Lilliput
10. K. Brobdingnag
11. H. Luggnagg
12. N. Munodi
13. J. Laputa
14. A. Houyhnhnms
15. E. Blefuscu

A. Food Gulliver ate with Houyhnhnms
B. Gulliver's name in Brobdingnag
C. Reasoning animals
D. Governor here called forth dead persons
E. Land of enemies of Lilliputians
F. Bestial man-like creature
G. Land with the Academy of Projectors
H. Gulliver licked the king's floor here
I. Word meaning "drink and be merry"
J. Floating island
K. Land of big people
L. Gulliver's "nurse" friend
M. People who live forever
N. Gulliver's friend in Lagado
O. Gulliver's enemy in Lilliput
P. Servants who hit their masters
Q. Land of little people

* Also use the above Matching answer key for the Multiple Choice Unit Test 2 and the Advanced Short Answer Test.

II. Short Answer

1. How did Gulliver help the Lilliputians against the Blefuscuians?

    He made cables with hooks, crossed the water, hooked the cables to the Blefuscuian ships and pulled them back to Lilliput.

2. The emperor of Lilliput wanted Gulliver to do more to help him finally crush the Blefuscuians so he could be emperor of all the lands. What was Gulliver's response?

    He protested that he would never be an instrument of bringing a free and brave people into slavery.

3. Describe the people of Brobdingnag.

    They were giants to Gulliver, about 60 feet tall.

4. What was the King of Brobdingnag's reaction to Gulliver's accounts of English manners, laws, religion, and government?

   He fell into a hearty fit of laughter and "observed how contemptible a thing was human grandeur, which could be mimicked by such diminutive insects as (Gulliver)."

5. What gift did Gulliver wish to give the King of Brobdingnag, and what was the King's reaction to the offer?

   Gulliver wanted to show him how to make and use gunpowder. The king was shocked by the uses of gunpowder and wanted nothing to do with it.

6. How did Gulliver describe the Laputians (physically and personality)?

   Their heads were inclined either to the right or the left; one eye was turned upward, and one was turned inward. They were clumsy, awkward, and unhappy. They were bad reasoners, vehemently given to opposition, and knew only about mathematics and music.

7. What were four of the projects Gulliver saw Professors attempting at the Academy of Projectors?

   a. One professor was trying to extract sunbeams from cucumbers.
   b. One professor was trying to reduce human excrement to its original food.
   c. One was trying to turn calcine ice into gunpowder.
   d. One was making a method for building houses from the roof down.
   e. A blind professor was teaching apprentices how to distinguish colors by feeling and smelling.
   f. One professor was ploughing fields with hogs instead of a plough.
   g. One was breeding spiders and silkworms to give different colored threads.
   h. One was a doctor who tried to cure ailments with bellows.
   i. One was breeding naked sheep.

8. How did most of the other residents of Luggnagg feel about the Struldbrugs?

   They are deprived and hated by most of the others.

9. What human concept was almost never heard of in the land of the Houyhnhnms?

   Lying, or saying "the thing which was not" was almost never heard of.

10. What effect did Gulliver's time with the Houyhnhnms have upon his view of his countrymen?

    He began to think the honor of his own kind not worth managing.

ADVANCED SHORT ANSWER TEST *Gulliver's Travels*

I. Matching

1. _____ Grildrig
2. _____ Lagado
3. _____ Flappers
4. _____ Glumdalclitch
5. _____ Glubbdubdrib
6. _____ Flimnap
7. _____ Yahoo
8. _____ Struldbrugs
9. _____ Lilliput
10. _____ Brobdingnag
11. _____ Luggnagg
12. _____ Munodi
13. _____ Laputa
14. _____ Houyhnhnms
15. _____ Blefuscu

A. Food Gulliver ate with Houyhnhnms
B. Gulliver's name in Brobdingnag
C. Reasoning animals
D. Governor here called forth dead persons
E. Land of enemies of Lilliputians
F. Bestial man-like creature
G. Land with the Academy of Projectors
H. Gulliver licked the king's floor here
I. Word meaning "drink and be merry"
J. Floating island
K. Land of big people
L. Gulliver's "nurse" friend
M. People who live forever
N. Gulliver's friend in Lagado
O. Gulliver's enemy in Lilliput
P. Servants who hit their masters
Q. Land of little people

II. Short Answer

1. Gulliver is quite a changed man after all his travels, when he sits down to write this book. What effects do his experiences have upon the way he relates his travels?

2. What comments does Swift (not Gulliver) make about religion in Gulliver's Travels? Use specific examples from the text to support your answers.

Gulliver Advanced Short Answer Unit Test page 2

3. Swift's views and Gulliver's views are often different. Explain how Swift uses Gulliver to make his points to us.

4. Explain the use of vice vs. virtue in *Gulliver's Travels*.

5. Explain how Gulliver's travels is a book about rational vs. irrational, and note the conclusions Swift would have us draw from his work.

6. What is irony? Give specific examples of Swift's use of irony, and explain the effects of the use of irony on us, the readers.

7. Gulliver is consumed with concern about what others think of him and his countrymen. give examples of this concern and explain its effect on his actions and on the themes of the book

Gulliver Advanced Short Answer Unit Test page 3

8. Explain Swift's (not Gulliver's) views on science. Use specific examples from the text to support your answers.

9. What effects did each of Gulliver's adventures have upon him?

10. Considering Gulliver's Travels, define "man" as you think Swift would. Use examples from the text to support your answers when possible.

Gulliver Advanced Short Answer Unit Test page 4

III. Essay

Considering all of Gulliver's travels, explain what Swift would consider an ideal race of beings, and explain why or why not man is or could become that race.

Gulliver Advanced Short Answer Unit Test page 5

IV. Vocabulary

Listen to the vocabulary words and write them down. Then write a composition using all of the words. The composition must relate in some way to *Gulliver's Travels*.

MULTIPLE CHOICE UNIT TEST 1 *Gulliver's Travels*

I. Matching

1. _____ Yahoo
2. _____ Lilliput
3. _____ Brobdingnag
4. _____ Blefuscu
5. _____ Glumdalclitch
6. _____ Houyhnhnms
7. _____ Laputa
8. _____ Flimnap
9. _____ Munodi
10. _____ Glubbdubdrib
11. _____ Luggnagg
12. _____ Flappers
13. _____ Grildrig
14. _____ Struldbrugs
15. _____ Lagado

A. Gulliver's friend in Lagado
B. Land with the Academy of Projectors
C. People who live forever
D. Gulliver's name in Brobdingnag
E. Floating island
F. Bestial man-like creature
G. Gulliver licked the king's floor here
H. Land of big people
I. Land of little people
J. Servants who hit their masters
K. Gulliver's "nurse" friend
L. Gulliver's enemy in Lilliput
M. Food Gulliver ate with Houyhnhnms
N. Word meaning "drink and be merry"
O. Governor here called forth dead persons
P. Reasoning animals
Q. Land of enemies of Lilliputians

II. Multiple Choice

1. What did the Lilliputians look like? (Book One--I-IV)
    A. They were about 24" high.
    B. They were about 6" high.
    C. They were about 15" high.
    D. They were about 3" high.

2. The Emperor delivered six Lilliputians who had attacked Gulliver to him for justice. What did he do with them? (Book One-I-IV)
    A. He threw them as far as he could, forcing them to walk all the way back to Lilliput.
    B. He put them in his pocket and pretended to eat them. Then he set them free.
    C. He gave them back to the Emperor and said he would abide by whatever course of action the Emperor wanted.
    D. He forced them to be his servants for day. They had to bring his food, comb his hair, and give him a bath.

Gulliver Multiple Choice Unit Test 1 page 2

3. About what are the Lilliputians and the Blefuscuians fighting? (Book One I-IV)
    A. They are fighting over who discovered their respective islands. Each group claims that one of their ancestors was the discoverer.
    B. They are fighting over whether to consolidate and become one large power or to stay two small powers. Opinions are about evenly divided.
    C. They are fighting over which end of the egg to break first. The Lilliputians break theirs on the little end and the Blefuscuians break theirs on the large end
    D. They are fighting over whether to use their dinner forks in the right or left hand. The Blefuscuians think it proper to hold the fork in the right hand, while the Lilliputians hold it in the left.

4. The Emperor wanted Gulliver to do more to help him finally crush the Blefuscuians. so he could be emperor of all the lands. What was Gulliver's response? (Book One V-VII)
    A. He agreed that "The stronger power should claim sovereignty over all the land."
    B. He "Plainly protested that he would never be an instrument of bringing a free and brave people into slavery."
    TWO CHOICES ONLY

5. In what ways did Gulliver profit from his adventure to Lilliput? (Book One V-VII)
    A. He wrote a book about his adventures and earned a great deal of money in royalties.
    B. He lectured to various groups and was paid well for the lectures.
    C. He had stolen a great deal of gold from both countries and was able to live comfortably on the income.
    D. He made a profit from showing and selling small animals.

6. What did the name "Grildrig" mean? (Book Two I-IV)
    A. It meant "Traveler."
    B. It meant "Mannikin."
    C. It meant "Handsome Little One."
    D. It meant "Curiosity."

7. What was the King's reaction to Gulliver's accounts of English manners, laws, religion, and government? (Book Two I-IV)
    A. He fell into a heart fit of laughing, and "observed how contemptible a thing was human grandeur, which could be mimicked by such diminutive insects as Gulliver.
    B. He somberly agreed that "sentient beings, regardless of size, all strove to maintain order and sensibility in their worlds."
    TWO CHOICES ONLY

Gulliver Multiple Choice Unit Test 1 page 3

8. Which was **not** one of the "ridiculous and troublesome accidents" that happened to Gulliver ? (Book Two V-VIII)
    A. Dwarf shook apples down from the tree onto Gulliver.
    B. He was beaten by hailstones.
    C. He was hit in the leg by a hazelnut.
    D. He was almost smothered when the Kite fell on him.

9. What was Gulliver's opinion of the learning of the people of Brobdingnag? (Book Two V-VIII)
    A. He thought they were extremely well-rounded.
    B. He thought their education was defective.
    TWO CHOICES ONLY

10. Which of the following statement describes the people Gulliver saw on the island of Laputa.? (Book Three I-V)
    A. They had two eyes on each side of their heads, but no mouths.
    B. Their heads were all inclined either to the right or to the left; one eye was turned inward, and the other was turned directly up.
    C. They had very long ear lobes, three nostrils, and teeth that protruded over their lips.
    D. Their facial features were the same on the front and the back, so that it was possible to talk to both sides of the person at the same time.

11. Some of the people who had been to the floating island learned a little about math and science and became satisfied with life on the ground when they returned. They began an institution "to put arts, sciences, languages, and mechanics on a new foot." What was the institution called? (Book Three I-V)
    A. It was called "The Institute for Learning."
    B. It was called "The Land Dwellers' University."
    C. It was called "The School for the Sciences and the Arts."
    D. It was called "The Academy of Projectors."

12. True or False: Gulliver called the political propositions "chimaeras" because they were such good, workable ideas. (Book Three VI-XI)
    A. True
    B. False

13. What did Gulliver conclude after seeing all the people who were brought back from the dead by the king of Glubbdubdrib? (Book Three VI-XI)
    A. Humans had made advances within the last hundred years.
    B. Humans had degenerated within the last hundred years."

Gulliver Multiple Choice Unit Test 1 page 4

14. What was the derivation of the word "Houyhnhnm" according to their language? (Book Four I-V)
    A. It meant "beast of burden."
    B. It meant "one who walks on four legs."
    C. It meant "of great intelligence."
    D. It meant "the perfection of nature."

15. How did Gulliver feel about humans after observing the Yahoos? (Book Four X-XII)
    A. He felt that humans were far superior to the Yahoos.
    B. He was ashamed to be a man.
    TWO CHOICES ONLY

Gulliver Multiple Choice Unit Test 1 page 5

III. Essay
Answer with a complete paragraph.

    Explain how *Gulliver's Travels* is a book about rational vs. irrational, and note the conclusions Swift would have us draw from his work.

Gulliver Multiple Choice Unit Test 1 page 6

IV. Vocabulary

1.	diminutive	A.	summarizing or repeating
2.	expostulate	B.	cannot be imitated or reproduced
3.	recompensed	C.	paid, made compensation for
4.	disapprobation	D.	needlessly repetitive
5.	insatiable	E.	disapproval
6.	mastiff	F.	descendants, succeeding generations
7.	ignominy	G.	to reason earnestly with someone
8.	battalia	H.	forecasting what is to come: predictions
9.	recapitulation	I.	small, tiny
10.	posterity	J.	conversation, formal discussion
11.	candour	K.	equality
12.	vehemence	L.	a stimulant
13.	discourse	M.	a feeling, show, or attitude of scornful superiority
14.	commodious	N.	sincerity, honesty
15.	redundant	O.	not able to be satisfied
16.	disdain	P.	dishonor, infamy
17.	provocative	Q.	spacious, roomy
18.	prognostics	R.	a large dog of ancient breed
19.	parity	S.	characterized by violence of feeling or endeavor
20.	inimitable	T.	an army in battle array or on the march

ANSWER SHEET Multiple Choice Unit Test 1 *Gulliver's Travels*

Name _____ Date _____ Class _____

I. Matching
1. _____
2. _____
3. _____
4. _____
5. _____
6. _____
7. _____
8. _____
9. _____
10. _____
11. _____
12. _____
13. _____
14. _____
15. _____

IV. Vocabulary
1. _____
2. _____
3. _____
4. _____
5. _____
6. _____
7. _____
8. _____
9. _____
10. _____
11. _____
12. _____
13. _____
14. _____
15. _____
16. _____
17. _____
18. _____
19. _____
20. _____

II Multiple Choice
1. (A) (B) (C) (D)
2. (A) (B) (C) (D)
3. (A) (B) (C) (D)
4. (A) (B) (C) (D)
5. (A) (B) (C) (D)
6. (A) (B) (C) (D)
7. (A) (B) (C) (D)
8. (A) (B) (C) (D)
9. (A) (B) (C) (D)
10. (A) (B) (C) (D)
11. (A) (B) (C) (D)
12. (A) (B) (C) (D)
13. (A) (B) (C) (D)
14. (A) (B) (C) (D)
15. (A) (B) (C) (D)

ANSWER KEY Multiple Choice Unit Test 1 *Gulliver's Travels*

I. Matching
1. F.
2. I.
3. H.
4. Q.
5. K.
6. P.
7. E.
8. L.
9. A.
10. O.
11. G.
12. J.
13. D.
14. C.
15. B.

IV. Vocabulary
1. I
2. G
3. C
4. E
5. O
6. R
7. P
8. T
9. A
10. F
11. N
12. S
13. J
14. Q
15. D
16. M
17. L
18. H
19. K
20. B

II. Multiple Choice
1. (A) ( ) (C) (D)
2. (A) ( ) (C) (D)
3. (A) (B) ( ) (D)
4. (A) ( ) (C) (D)
5. (A) (B) (C) ( )
6. (A) ( ) (C) (D)
7. ( ) (B) (C) (D)
8. (A) (B) ( ) (D)
9. (A) ( ) (C) (D)
10. (A) ( ) (C) (D)
11. (A) (B) (C) ( )
12. (A) ( ) (C) (D)
13. (A) ( ) (C) (D)
14. (A) (B) (C) ( )
15. (A) ( ) (C) (D)

MULTIPLE CHOICE UNIT TEST 2 *Gulliver's Travels*

I. Matching

1. _____ Grildrig
2. _____ Lagado
3. _____ Flappers
4. _____ Glumdalclitch
5. _____ Glubbdubdrib
6. _____ Flimnap
7. _____ Yahoo
8. _____ Struldbrugs
9. _____ Lilliput
10. _____ Brobdingnag
11. _____ Luggnagg
12. _____ Munodi
13. _____ Laputa
14. _____ Houyhnhnms
15. _____ Blefuscu

A. Food Gulliver ate with Houyhnhnms
B. Gulliver's name in Brobdingnag
C. Reasoning animals
D. Governor here called forth dead persons
E. Land of enemies of Lilliputians
F. Bestial man-like creature
G. Land with the Academy of Projectors
H. Gulliver licked the king's floor here
I. Word meaning "drink and be merry"
J. Floating island
K. Land of big people
L. Gulliver's "nurse" friend
M. People who live forever
N. Gulliver's friend in Lagado
O. Gulliver's enemy in Lilliput
P. Servants who hit their masters
Q. Land of little people

II. Multiple Choice

1. How is the story told? (Book One--I-IV)
   a. It is told in the first person by the ship's doctor.
   b. It is told in the second person in the form of letters from the first mate to his wife.
   c. It is told in the third person by a nephew of the traveler.
   d. It is told through the diary of the ship's captain.

2. What are the two political factions in Lilliput? (Book One I-IV)
   a. They are the Pointed Ears and the Rounded Ears.
   b. They are the High Heels and the Low Heels.
   c. They are the Long Hairs and the Short Hairs.
   d. They are the Soft Voices and the Loud Voices.

3. How did Gulliver escape from Lilliput? (Book One V-VII)
   a. He stepped on the armory and destroyed all of their weapons.
   b. He held the Emperor hostage until the Lilliputians agreed to leave him alone.
   c. He swam to Blefuscu.
   d. He stood on top of their highest mountain and threatened to hurl rocks at the town unless they treated him better.

Gulliver Multiple Choice Unit Test 2 page 2

4. Give a brief physical description of the residents of Brobdingnag.(Book Two I-IV)
	a. They were the same size as Gulliver.
	b. They were smaller than Gulliver, but larger than the Lilliputians.
	c. They were about 15 feet tall.
	d. They were giants, about 60 feet tall.

5. After Gulliver took great pride in telling the King about England over the period of about a week, what was the King's reaction? Book Two V-VIII)
	a. He asked Gulliver to take him there for a visit.
	b. He said he was glad he was not an Englishman.
	c. He expressed his displeasure with the country and the people.
	d. He felt envious of the superiority of the English.

6. What gift did Gulliver wish to give the King so the King would have a more favorable impression of him? (Book Two V-VIII)
	a. Gulliver showed him a Bible and offered to teach him to read English.
	b. Gulliver offered him several gold crowns.
	c. Gulliver offered the King a year's worth of service.
	d. Gulliver offered to show the King how to make and use gunpowder.

7. What was the Captain's, and then Gulliver's wife's reaction to his behavior when they first encountered him after his journey? (Book Two V-VIII)
	a. They thought he had lost his wits.
	b. They thought he had learned a lot.
	c. They thought he was just the same as when he left.
	d. They thought his disposition was much improved

8. Which of the following does **not** describe the Laputians? (Book Three I-V)
	a. They were clumsy, awkward and unhappy.
	b. They were bad reasoners.
	c. They were vehemently given to opposition.
	d. They were very weak in mathematics and musical abilities.

Gulliver Multiple Choice Unit Test 2 page 3

9. Which of the following was not one of the projects Gulliver saw the Professors attempting? (Book Three I-V)
    a. One professor was trying to extract sunbeams from cucumbers.
    b. One professor was trying to reduce human excrement to its original food.
    c. One professor was trying to turn calcium carbonate into paper that could be written on and then eaten.
    d. One professor was making a method for building houses from the roof down.

10. Why did Gulliver go to Luggnagg? (Book Three VI-XI)
    a. He was taken there against his will by the captain of the boat.
    b. He wanted to write a book about the country.
    c. He would be able to find a ship to Japan, and then find a ship to England.
    d. He thought he could become the ruler, because he and heard there was inner turmoil and the people wanted a strong leader.

11. How did most of the other residents feel about the Struldbrugs? (Book Three VI-XI)
    a. They envied their immortality.
    b. They hated the Struldbrugs.
    c. Most of the people felt compassion towards them and their unusual circumstances.
    d. Since the identities of the Struldbrugs were kept secret, most people didn't even know who they were, and so ignored them.

12. Why was Gulliver's "master" so eager to teach him the language of the Houyhnhnms? (Book Four I-V)
    a. He wanted Gulliver to be able to teach him to speak English.
    b. He wanted to train Gulliver to perform menial tasks.
    c. He wanted to learn about Gulliver, and to understand him.
    d. He wanted to learn where Gulliver came from, because he wanted to send an army there to conquer the people.

Gulliver Multiple Choice Unit Test 2 page 4

13. Gulliver and his master had several discussions. To what subject does the following quotation refer?
"...But when a creature pretending to reason could be capable of such enormities, he dreaded lest the corruption of that faculty might be worse than brutality itself. He seemed therefore confident. that instead of reason, we were only possessed of some quality fitted to increase our natural vices: as the reflection from a troubled stream returns the image of an ill-shapen body, not only larger, but more distorted." (Book Four I-V)
    a. They were discussing the concept of sin.
    b. They were discussing the concept of war.
    c. They were discussing the concept of money.
    d. They were discussing the concept of death.

14. Why did Gulliver feel he could no longer deny he was a real Yahoo? (Book Four VI-IX)
    a. He enjoyed the same food as they did.
    b. He preferred their company to that of the Houyhnhnms.
    c. A female Yahoo showed her attraction to him.
    d. His thoughts and actions were similar to theirs.

15. What was Gulliver's reaction to his family and countrymen upon his return from the land of the Houyhnhnms? (Book Four VI-IX)
    a. He embraced them and vowed never to leave again.
    b. He rejected them.
    TWO CHOICES ONLY

Gulliver Multiple Choice Unit Test 2 page 5

III. Essay
Answer with a complete paragraph.

Compare and contrast views on war in each of the lands Gulliver visited, and explain Swift's (not Gulliver's) comment on the subject of war.

Gulliver Multiple Choice Unit Test 2 page 6

IV. Vocabulary

1.	prodigious	A.	read, scrutinized
2.	animosities	B.	defended, set free, avenged
3.	expedient	C.	conducive to a result
4.	alacrity	D.	carefully conforming to the dictates of conscience
5.	extenuations	E.	briskness, cheerful readiness
6.	pursuant	F.	sincerity, honesty
7.	edifice	G.	bitter hostilities, hatred
8.	erudition	H.	an expression of general truth
9.	perused	I.	extraordinary size, amount, etc.
10.	candour	J.	closed so as to be air tight
11.	vehemence	K.	attributed to
12.	conjecture	L.	without distinctive, interesting, or attractive qualities; dull
13.	hermetically	M.	beat of any rhythmical movement
14.	licentiousness	N.	characterized by violence of feeling or endeavor; passionate
15.	scrupulous	O.	partial excuses
16.	cadence	P.	a building, especially of a large size
17.	insipid	Q.	unrestrained by law or morality
18.	maxim	R.	proceeding comfortably
19.	imputed	S.	to infer from inconclusive evidence
20.	vindicated	T.	learning, scholarship, knowledge

ANSWER SHEET Multiple Choice Unit Test 2 *Gulliver's Travels*

Name _____ Date _____ Class _____

I. Matching

1. _____
2. _____
3. _____
4. _____
5. _____
6. _____
7. _____
8. _____
9. _____
10. _____
11. _____
12. _____
13. _____
14. _____
15. _____

IV. Vocabulary

1. _____
2. _____
3. _____
4. _____
5. _____
6. _____
7. _____
8. _____
9. _____
10. _____
11. _____
12. _____
13. _____
14. _____
15. _____
16. _____
17. _____
18. _____
19. _____
20. _____

II. Multiple Choice

1. (A) (B) (C) (D)
2. (A) (B) (C) (D)
3. (A) (B) (C) (D)
4. (A) (B) (C) (D)
5. (A) (B) (C) (D)
6. (A) (B) (C) (D)
7. (A) (B) (C) (D)
8. (A) (B) (C) (D)
9. (A) (B) (C) (D)
10. (A) (B) (C) (D)
11. (A) (B) (C) (D)
12. (A) (B) (C) (D)
13. (A) (B) (C) (D)
14. (A) (B) (C) (D)
15. (A) (B) (C) (D)

ANSWER KEY Multiple Choice Unit Test 2 *Gulliver's Travels*

I. Matching
1. B.
2. G.
3. P.
4. L.
5. D.
6. O.
7. F.
8. M.
9. Q.
10. K.
11. H.
12. N.
13. J.
14. A.
15. E.

IV. Vocabulary
1. I.
2. G.
3. C.
4. E.
5. O.
6. R.
7. P.
8. T.
9. A.
10. F.
11. N.
12. S.
13. J.
14. Q.
15. D.
16. M.
17. L.
18. H.
19. K.
20. B.

II. Multiple Choice
1. ( ) (B) (C) (D)
2. (A) ( ) (C) (D)
3. (A) (B) ( ) (D)
4. (A) (B) (C) ( )
5. (A) ( ) (C) (D)
6. (A) (B) (C) ( )
7. ( ) (B) (C) (D)
8. (A) (B) (C) ( )
9. (A) (B) ( ) (D)
10. (A) (B) ( ) (D)
11. (A) ( ) (C) (D)
12. (A) (B) ( ) (D)
13. (A) ( ) (C) (D)
14. (A) (B) ( ) (D)
15. (A) ( ) (C) (D)

UNIT RESOURCE MATERIALS

EXTRA ACTIVITIES

One of the difficulties in teaching a novel is that all students don't read at the same speed. One student who likes to read may take the book home and finish it in a day or two. Sometimes a few students finish the in-class assignments early. The problem, then, is finding suitable extra activities for students.

One thing that helps is to keep a little library in the classroom. For this unit on *Gulliver's Travels*, you might check out from the school or public library other books by Jonathan Swift. A biography of Swift would be interesting for some students. You can include other related books and articles about sailing, the history of England during Swift's life (1667-1745), scientific and technological inventions, or articles of criticism about *Gulliver's Travels*..

Other things you may keep on hand are word search puzzles. Several puzzles relating directly to *Gulliver's Travels* are included in the unit. Feel free to duplicate them.

Some students may like to draw. You might devise a contest or allow some extra-credit grade for students who draw characters or scenes from Gulliver's Travels. Note, too, that if the students do not want to keep their drawings you may pick up some extra bulletin board materials this way. If you have a contest and you supply the prize. You could, possibly, make the drawing itself a non-refundable entry fee.

The pages which follow contain games, puzzles, and worksheets. The keys, when appropriate, immediately follow the puzzle or worksheet. There are two main groups of activities: one group for the the unit: that is, generally relating to the Gulliver's Travles text, and another group of activities relates strictly to the *Gulliver's Travels* vocabulary.

Directions for the games, puzzles, and worksheets are self-explanatory. The object here is to provide you with extra materials you may use in any way you choose.

MORE ACTIVITIES *Gulliver's Travels*

1. Pick a chapter or scene with a great deal of dialogue and have the students act it out. (Perhaps you could assign various scenes to different groups of students so more than one scene could be acted and more students could participate.)

2. Show a film version of *Gulliver's Travels* after you have completed reading the novel. Have students evaluate the movie and compare/contrast it with the book. If the students have tried writing a chapter into a scene in a play, you may wish to discuss how the problems they encountered in changing the form were handled in the movie.

3. Have students design a book cover (front and back and inside flaps) for *Gulliver's Travels*.

4. Have students design a bulletin board (ready to be put up; not just sketched) for *Gulliver's Travels*.

5. Have a guest speaker talk about their travels, especially what it feels like to be a stranger in another place..

6. Use some of the related topics (noted earlier for an in-class library) as topics for research, reports, or written papers, or as topics for guest speakers.

7. Have a talk show. The host will interview Gulliver, who has recently returned from one of his journeys. (Students should make up the questions they want the host to ask Gulliver.) A few inhabitants of the various countries could also be on the talk show.

8. Have a talk show. The host will interview Gulliver's wife and children. They should tell what their lives are like when Gulliver is away, and how it changes when he returns.

9. Use graph paper and have students make scale models of the Lilliputians, Gulliver, and the Brobdingnagians for comparison.

10. Invite students who have read other books about fantastic travels to give short book talks, and compare and contrast Gulliver's experiences with those of the other characters.

11. Design a new land for Gulliver to visit. Describe the people, the location of the country, and the physical characteristics of the country. Describe the views on politics, education, government, and war.

12. Brainstorm ways for Gulliver to use his time now that his journeys have come to an end.

13. *Gulliver's Travels* was intended to be a satire of the time in which it was written. Have students research England at that time, and find out exactly what was being satirized.

BULLETIN BOARD IDEAS *Gulliver's Travels*

1. Save one corner of the board for the best of students' Gulliver's Travels writing assignments.

2. Take one of the word search puzzles from the extra activities packet and with a marker copy it over in a large size on the bulletin board. Write the clue words to find to one side. Invite students prior to and after class to find the words and circle them on the bulletin board. Cut out letters to title the board, "A SEARCH FOR *Gulliver's Travels*."

3. Make a travel bulletin board of interesting places the modern traveller can visit -- exotic lands and far-away places. (Your local travel agent should have loads of great pictures, etc. for you.)

4. Make a bulletin board about inventions through the years -- things which have proven to be useful, or more appropriately, things which never have found a use at all.

5. Post articles of criticism about Gulliver's Travels.

6. Post a world map and mark on it the approximate site of each of Gulliver's adventures.

7. Do a bulletin board about different, interesting cultures which exist in the world today. One easy way to do this is to post articles and pictures from National Geographic magazine.

8. Find quotes from philosophers, theologians and other famous people about the nature of man, religion, science, and educations. Display them on a bulletin board.

9. Provide blank index cards and markers. Invite students to design postcards Gulliver could have sent. Display them on the board.

Word Search *Gulliver's Travels*

```
G O L V S Q U E E N H S T F P A N M I L F O B K C F A U
E U K U I O U S P E C X T A Y A H O O G E R R F I D T R
O J L I G C D F W A W O F R E P P A L F O E B O V N R O
C A Z L T G E A F I C B R M U G Z U M B V L I E Y R G B
O P E H I E N D B S F S L E E L B V D I R R N L M A E S
U A D C K V W A T R P T E R J B D I R L S T I A E M X U
L N N T L O E O G I A S X D D P N B A G U E C N D V M C
M K E I L O R R R G R B H U B G I P R R Y A L G A R C D
E S M L O M A A S O G T B E N S U Z E U P C L U C B P J
M P A C R A T T H T O D S A E T O D H T G A E A A D O G
K W S L B E T P S S R D G K A L W U A R F S W G W P R I
S L I A S O O N X I C A A G U N R I J O W Z E E D I E C
Y I I D T L D M B Q C O V G J E N D P T E Q P W W H E O
U Y Y M R O N R E V O G H E A L I A S V Y C O U A S L U
F H O U Y H N H N M S V G S L L M C A T L S H O R S G N
G R I L D R I G Y X A Z O W O S B L E F U S C U F W P C
A H O G M U T I N Y N N K C U N K C A L P S G M H G Z I
I D O N U M B A T E S L I L L I P U T R M D N A L S I L
```

BROBDINGNAG	GOVERNOR	BLEFUSCU	YAHOO
GULLIVERS TRAVELS	LILLIPUT	LANGUAGE	WASP
STRULDBRUGS	PIRATES	DWARF	SAIL
GLUMDALCLITCH	BARBADOS	ACADEMY	SEA
SWALLOW	COUNCIL	FLAPPER	HAY
LAGADO	MUNODI	QUEEN	OATS
GRILDRIG	MUTINY	FARMER	VICE
REASON	CAPTAIN	KING	SHIP
STORM	SPLACKNUCK	MENDEZZ	GUN
ESCAPE	JAPAN	LAPUTA	CAT
HORSE	ADVENTURE	BATES	RAT
ISLAND	HOPEWELL	KITE	MILK
HOUYHNHNMS	FLIMNAP	SWIFT	RIVER
GLUBBDUBDRIB	HEEL	BOX	EGG
LUGGNAGG			

CROSSWORD *Gulliver's Travels*

CROSSWORD CLUES *Gulliver's Travels*

ACROSS
4 Articles of treason against Gulliver
7 Thought Gulliver was its young one
10 Worst crime in Lilliput
12 Servants who hit their masters
14 Ship that was attacked by pirates
17 Proper way to break them was disputed in Lilliput
18 Animal of Brobdingnag
19 Gulliver licked the king's floor there
23 Displayed Gulliver to make money
25 Land of little people
26 Gulliver's wife
27 Rebellious city in Laputa
28 Gulliver's name in Brobdingnag

DOWN
1 Captain who found Gulliver near Blefuscu
2 Continent under Laputa
3 Heels currently in power in Lilliput
5 Academy trying new methods
6 Reasoning animals
8 Bird that carried Gulliver's box out to sea
9 Fond of Gulliver's company in Brobdingnag
11 Floating island
12 Gulliver's enemy in Lilliput
13 Man's worst vice, according to Gulliver
15 Set Gulliver adrift in a sloop
16 People who live forever
18 Author of *Gulliver's Travels*
20 Wrote about his adventures
21 Houyhnhnm council meeting: ___ Assembly
22 Bestial man-like creature
24 Gulliver's homeland
25 None done in land of Houyhnhnms
26 Unpleasant company for Gulliver: ___ of Honor

CROSSWORD ANSWER KEY *Gulliver's Travels*

MATCHING QUIZ / WORKSHEET 1 *Gulliver's Travels*

___ 1. Gulliver   A. break eggs on little end
___ 2. Lilliputians   B. nimble, good swimmers
___ 3. Blefuscuians   C. clumsy, unhappy people
___ 4. laborers   D. showed Gulliver off for money
___ 5. farmer   E. found Gulliver in Brobdingnag
___ 6. pirates   F. ideas at Academy of Projectors
___ 7. flappers   G. friendly, benevolent, gentle
___ 8. Laputians   H. only Europeans permitted in Japan
___ 9. blind professor   I. narrator of story
___ 10. Hannibal and Caesar   J. debating the fate of the Yahoos
___ 11. Dutch   K. hit masters to draw their attention
___ 12. impossible chimaeras   L. set Gulliver adrift in a canoe
___ 13. Luggnagg   M. home of Struldbrugs
___ 14. Adventure   N. distinguishing colors by feel and smell
___ 15. magicians   O. required strange means of address
___ 16. Yahoos   P. crew mutinied and set Gulliver ashore
___ 17. Grand Assembly   Q. recalled from dead in Glubbdubdrib
___ 18. Swift   R. break eggs on large end
___ 19. Houyhnhnms   S. Gulliver's first impression of Houyhnhnms
___ 20. King of Luggnagg   T. author of novel

ANSWER KEY   MATCHING QUIZ / WORKSHEET 1 Gulliver's Travels

I	1.	Gulliver	A.	break eggs on little end
A	2.	Lilliputians	B.	nimble, good swimmers
R	3.	Blefuscuians	C.	clumsy, unhappy people
E	4.	laborers	D.	showed Gulliver off for money
D	5.	farmer	E.	found Gulliver in Brobdingnag
L	6.	pirates	F.	ideas at Academy of Projectors
K	7.	flappers	G.	friendly, benevolent, gentle
C	8.	Laputians	H.	only Europeans permitted in Japan
N	9.	blind professor	I.	narrator of story
Q	10.	Hannibal and Caesar	J.	debating the fate of the Yahoos
H	11.	Dutch	K.	hit masters to draw their attention
F	12.	impossible chimaeras	L.	set Gulliver adrift in a canoe
M	13.	Luggnagg	M.	home of Struldbrugs
P	14.	Adventure	N.	distinguishing colors by fee land smell
S	15.	magicians	O.	required strange means of address
B	16.	Yahoos	P.	crew mutinied and set Gulliver ashore
J	17.	Grand Assembly	Q.	recalled from dead in Glubbdubdrib
T	18.	Swift	R.	break eggs on large end
G	19.	Houyhnhnms	S.	Gulliver's first impression of Houyhnhnms
O	20.	King of Luggnagg	T.	author of novel

MATCHING QUIZ /WORKSHEET 2 *Gulliver's Travels*

___ 1. ancient temple   A. political factions in Lilliput

___ 2. High and Low Heels   B. total number of Gulliver's voyages

___ 3. Gulliver's thumb   C. used to hit distracted Laputians

___ 4. 1728   D. Gulliver ate as much food as this many Lilliputians

___ 5. *Adventure*   E. total years and months of Gulliver's voyages

___ 6. 60   F. Gulliver's means of departure from Houyhnhnmland

___ 7. Japanese Captain   G. height of Brobdingnagians in feet

___ 8. 5 : 6   H. length of time of Gulliver's third voyage (yrs & months)

___ 9. floating island   I. wore garments adorned with moons and stars

___ 10. self-made boat   J. Gulliver's dwelling in Laputa

___ 11. bird   K. used to determine his measurements

___ 12. *Swallow*   L. took Gulliver from Brobdingnag

___ 13. 4   M. rebellious city of Laputa

___ 14. 16:7   N. Gulliver's dwelling in Lilliput

___ 15. Laputians   O. took Gulliver to Lilliput

___ 16. Grildrig   P. Gulliver's name in Brobdingnag

___ 17. wooden box or closet   Q. left Gulliver in Brobdingnag

___ 18. bladder of pebbles   R. captured by pirates

___ 19. Lindalino   S. set Gulliver adrift in a canoe

___ 20. Hopewell   T. Gulliver's dwelling in Brobdingnag

ANSWER KEY MATCHING QUIZ /WORKSHEET 2 *Gulliver's Travels*

N	1.	ancient temple	A.	political factions in Lilliput
A	2.	High and Low Heels	B.	total number of Gulliver's voyages
K	3.	Gulliver's thumb	C.	used to hit distracted Laputians
D	4.	1728	D.	Gulliver ate as much food as this many Lilliputians
Q	5.	*Adventure*	E.	total years and months of Gulliver's voyages
G	6.	60	F.	Gulliver's means of departure from Houyhnhnmland
S	7.	Japanese Captain	G.	height of Brobdingnagians in feet
H	8.	5 : 6	H.	length of time of Gulliver's third voyage (yrs & months)
J	9.	floating island	I.	wore garments adorned with moons and stars
F	10.	self-made boat	J.	Gulliver's dwelling in Laputa
L	11.	bird	K.	used to determine his measurements
O	12.	*Swallow*	L.	took Gulliver from Brobdingnag
B	13.	4	M.	rebellious city of Laputa
E	14.	16:7	N.	Gulliver's dwelling in Lilliput
I	15.	Laputians	O.	took Gulliver to Lilliput
P	16.	Grildrig	P.	Gulliver's name in Brobdingnag
T	17.	wooden box or closet	Q.	left Gulliver in Brobdingnag
C	18.	bladder of pebbles	R.	captured by pirates
M	19.	Lindalino	S.	set Gulliver adrift in a canoe
R	20.	*Hopewell*	T.	Gulliver's dwelling in Brobdingnag

JUGGLE LETTER REVIEW GAME CLUE SHEET *Gulliver's Travels*

BNBABIRAIL	BALNIBARBI	Continent under Laputa
DIBLED	BIDDLE	Captain who found Gulliver near Blefuscu
EUCSUBFIL	BLEFUSCU	Land of enemies of Lilliput
DBGBAOGNNIR	BROBDINGNAG	Land of big people
UTHDC	DUTCH	Only Europeans allowed in Japan
GESG	EGGS	Proper way to break was disputed in Lilliput
GDNNALE	ENGLAND	Gulliver's home
RITTENEEXAM	EXTERMINATE	Houyhnhnm plan for Yahoos
RERAFM	FARMER	Displayed Gulliver to make money
PRESFAPL	FLAPPERS	Servants who hit their masters
MINPFAL	FLIMNAP	Gulliver's enemy in Lilliput
ADFUR	FRAUD	Worst crime in Lilliput
DUBLGBURDIBU	GLUBBDUBDRIB	Governor here called forth dead persons
ULIGLCLCMHTDA	GLUMDALCLITCH	Gulliver's "little nurse"
GAMESBRYDSNAL	GRAND ASSEMBLY	Houyhnhnm council meeting
LIVRGLUE	GULLIVER	Wrote about his adventures
PWUDRNGEO	GUNPOWDER	King of Brobdingnag refused this gift
WOLEHELP	HOPEWELL	Ship that was attacked by pirates
OHHSNUYMHN	HOUYHNHNMS	Reasoning animals
ECMINHEMTAP	IMPEACHMENT	Articles of treason against Gulliver
TEIK	KITE	Bird that carried Gulliver's box out to sea
PLATAU	LAPUTA	Floating island
ILULTPLI	LILLIPUT	land of little people
DLIONLIAN	LINDALINO	Rebellious city in Laputa
OEWSLLHE	LOW HEELS	Currently in power in Lilliput
GUAGGNGL	LUGGNAGG	Gulliver licked the king's floor here
YGINL	LYING	Not done in land of Houyhnhnms
FMSORAOOHINP	MAIDS OF HONOR	Unpleasant company for Gulliver
ANNIMINK	MANNIKIN	Gulliver's name in Brobdingnag
YUTNAORMBR	MARY BURTON	Gulliver's wife
YMNEOK	MONKEY	Thought Gulliver was its young one
NOMIUD	MUNODI	Gulliver's friend in Lagado
RPSETIA	PIRATES	Set Gulliver adrift in a sloop
EIRDP	PRIDE	Man's worst vice, according to Gulliver
RCOESTORPJ	PROJECTORS	Academy trying new methods
NEQEU	QUEEN	Fond of Gulliver's company in Brobdingnag

PAKCNKLUCS	SPLACKNUCK	Animal of Brobdingnag
UGTRDUSSBLR	STRULDBRUGS	People who live forever
FITWS	SWIFT	Author of Gulliver's travels
OHAOY	YAHOO	Bestial man-like creature

VOCABULARY RESOURCES

VOCABULARY WORD SEARCH 1 *Gulliver's Travels*

All words in this list are associated with *Gulliver's Travels*.. The words are placed backwards, forward, diagonally, up and down. The clues below the word search can help you find the words.

```
N Q V S O G R T Z C D E Y N M V Z O C W V F S V F R U I A S Z
F I V H J V I P O N I L T O E N E A O U U M J Y E E R Q S J F
P Q A P C I E N L I S B I I E C V H Q U S U T T L C D L X B D
S J N D B M J H T N A A S T H M N S E I L I Y V I O K S W L W
F Q W B S E L N N X P R N A I G Z A H M D F H Q C M L G D S N
C L Q O C I A F G H P E E L Y I V C N I E I H T I P E O A L R
R G M T Y U D K P Y R P P L U N S F P E A N E Z T E M P T I U
Y E U P S I G I T U O U O E D N I E K F T W C Z Y N S K R R A
Z R C R N P O B D B B S R P W D R A K F R N C E T S U R N I I
I B U A E H A I D A A N P P X T P N L I G E U L H E P G L L C
F P H T P X T D S Q T I E A N U O I E T H N D O E D E A W A D
T Z S M S I O I J S I V Z I V N S M R S G Q Q U C M T T N R E
H N U M O I T E T O O J L J E U T O C A R A Z Q N T E D N O T
A D E N O X E U H G N Y L F K U E S M M U U Q J A D O N R I A
U U J I Z W Q A L A C R I T Y F R I F X U Y O B N U A C C V C
B N A I D I Z N J A R B V X A L I T T E J T W C R Q I N G Y I
S B Q P U E B A H X T K E U H P T I U X O W W Q S Z N G T K D
H D B A G G P G T I N E Z O H M Y E B O X E P I H I H H M S N
A N S D Z S G X D E C L I V I T Y S U O Q M H D H X D H S I I
T V Q V W U E N E Q R C O N F E D E R A C Y Q T A U C U D X V
```

DECLIVITY	PURSUANT	ZENITH
INTREPIDITY	SCHISMS	REDUNDANT
CLEMENCY	BATTALIA	APPELLATION
ANIMOSITIES	RECAPITULATE	DISDAIN
EXPEDIENT	ERUDITION	INSUPERABLE
RECOMPENSED	POSTERITY	VINDICATED
COUNTENANCE	CANDOUR	PROPENSITY
DISAPPROBATION	VEHEMENCE	FELICITY
ALACRITY	CONJECTURE	CONFEDERACY
MASTIFF	DISCOURSE	

VOCABULARY CROSSWORD *Gulliver's Travels*

VOCABULARY CROSSWORD CLUES *Gulliver's Travels*

ACROSS
1 Pertaining to day
3 Wood or thicket of small trees and bushes
5 Sail near the stern of a 3-masted vessel
7 Manners, etc. of a foolish person
12 Cannot be imitated or reproduced; matchless
14 One who lives withdrawn from the world
17 Mercy
20 Having to do with spring
25 Large cask
28 Predatory bird having a long, forked tail
29 Equality
30 Dull; without interesting qualitites
31 Divisions into mutually opposed parties
32 Infer from inconclusive evidence

DOWN
2 Discrediting or degrading
4 Proceeding from and conformable to; in accordance with
5 Axiom; an expression of a general truth
6 Highest point; culmination
8 Hateful or detestable; obnoxious
9 Horse of reddish-brown color
10 Magic; conjuration
11 Set free; defended; avenged
13 Unrestrained by law or morality; beyond proper limits
15 Trellis or framework on which trees or shrubs are trained to grow in a flattened form
16 Equipped with trappings, accessories
18 Learning; scholarship; knowledge
19 Act of giving urgent advice or admonition as to conduct
21 Units of distance, each equal to 3 miles
22 Characterized by violence of feeling or endeavor; passion
23 An army in battle array or on the march
24 Feeling, attitude, or show of scornful superiority
26 Give sworn testimony; to lay aside; remove from office
27 Read; scrutinized

VOCABULARY CROSSWORD ANSWER KEY *Gulliver's Travels*

VOCABULARY WORKSHEET 1 *Gulliver's Travels*

___ 1. depose   A. to infer from inconclusive evidence
___ 2. rudiments   B. a mistake or oversight
___ 3. exhortation   C. magic or conjuration
___ 4. propensity   D. defended, avenged
___ 5. inimitable   E. natural inclination or tendency
___ 6. vindicated   F. the highest point
___ 7. disdain   G. descendants
___ 8. maxim   H. a show of scornful superiority
___ 9. redundant   I. small, tiny
___ 10. inadvertence   J. act of giving urgent advice
___ 11. necromancy   K. beginnings
___ 12. vehemence   L. summarizing or repeating
___ 13. zenith   M. cannot be imitated or reproduced
___ 14. conjecture   N. dishonor, infamy
___ 15. hermetically   O. give sworn testimony
___ 16. recapitulation P. an expression of general truth
___ 17. posterity   Q. closed so as to be air tight
___ 18. ignominy   R. needlessly repetitive
___ 19. impeachment   S. characterized by violence of feeling or endeavor
___ 20. diminutive   T. discredited or degraded

ANSWER KEY VOCABULARY WORKSHEET 1 *Gulliver's Travels*

O	1.	depose	A.	to infer from inconclusive evidence
K	2.	rudiments	B.	a mistake or oversight
J	3.	exhortation	C.	magic or conjuration
E	4.	propensity	D.	defended, avenged
M	5.	inimitable	E.	natural inclination or tendency
D	6.	vindicated	F.	the highest point
H	7.	disdain	G.	descendants
P	8.	maxim	H.	a show of scornful superiority
R	9.	redundant	I.	small, tiny
B	10.	inadvertence	J.	act of giving urgent advice
C	11.	necromancy	K.	beginnings
S	12.	vehemence	L.	summarizing or repeating
F	13.	zenith	M.	cannot be imitated or reproduced
A	14.	conjecture	N.	dishonor, infamy
Q	15.	hermetically	O.	give sworn testimony
L	16.	recapitulation	P.	an expression of general truth
G	17.	posterity	Q.	closed so as to be air tight
N	18.	ignominy	R.	needlessly repetitive
T	19.	impeachment	S.	characterized by violence of feeling or endeavor
I	20.	diminutive	T.	discredited or degraded

VOCABULARY WORKSHEET 2 *Gulliver's Travels*

_____ 1. a sloping downward

A. declivity   B. quadrant   C. edifice   D. trencher

_____ 2. mercy

A. animosities   B. alacrity   C. candour   D. clemency

_____ 3. caution, heedfulness

A. countenance   B. circumspection   C. schism   D. erudition

_____ 4. a trellis or framework on which trees are trained to grow in a flattened form

A. raillery   B. kite   C. sorrel   D. espalier

_____ 5. carefully conforming to the dictates of conscience

A. scrupulous   B. licentiousness   C. odious   D. commodious

_____ 6. catering to the baser passions of others

A. necromancy   B. orthography   C. panderism   D. erudition

_____ 7. a name or a title

A. maxim   B. appellation   C. circumlocution   D. allusion

_____ 8. descendants, succeeding generations

A. ignominy   B. intrepidity   C. posterity   D. propensity

_____ 9. a league or alliance

A. confederacy   B. copse   C. diurnal   D. schism

_____ 10. a flat piece of wood on which meat is carved and served

A. battalia   B. mizzen   C. mastiff   d. trencher

_____ 11. an indirect reference, casual mention

A. candour   B. allusion   c. interposition   d. exhortation

_____ 12. banter, good-humored ridicule

A. posterity   B. espalier   C. raillery   d. fopperies

_____ 13. a predatory bird having a long, forked tail

A. kite   B. trencher   C. edifice   D. sorrel

_____ 14. of extraordinary size or amount

A. diminutive   B. consummate   C. prodigious   D. insipid

_____ 15. deserving shame or disgrace

A. ignominious   B. disapprobation   C. insatiable   D. erudition

_____ 16. read, scrutinized

A. debauched   B. perused   C. vindicated   D. accoutred

_____ 17. fashion at a particular time; current use

A. comeliness   B. rudiments   C. parity   d. vogue

_____ 18. one who lives withdrawn from the world

A. copse   B. auditor   C. recluse   D. mastiff

_____ 19. without dignity or aspirations

A. grovelling   B. recompensed   C. expedient   D. scrofulous

_____ 20. hateful or detestable; obnoxious

A. vernal   B. inviolable   C. scrupulous   D. odious

ANSWER KEY   VOCABULARY WORKSHEET 2   Gulliver's Travels

A.   1. a sloping downward
   A. declivity   B. quadrant   C. edifice   D. trencher

D.   2. mercy
   A. animosities   B. alacrity   C. candour   D. clemency

B.   3. caution, heedfulness
   A. countenance   B. circumspection   C. schism   D. erudition

D.   4. a trellis or framework on which trees are trained to grow in a flattened form
   A. raillery   B. kite   C. sorrel   D. espalier

C.   5. carefully conforming to the dictates of conscience
   A. commodious   B. inadvertence   C. scrupulous   D. animosities

C.   6. catering to the baser passions of others
   A. necromancy   B. orthography   C. panderism   D. erudition

B.   7. a name or a title
   A. maxim   B. appellation   C. circumlocution   D. allusion

C.   8. descendants, succeeding generations
   A. ignominy   B. intrepidity   C. posterity   D. propensity

A.   9. a league or alliance
   A. confederacy   B. copse   C. diurnal   D. schism

D   10. a flat piece of wood on which meat is carved and served
   A. battalia   B. mizzen   C. mastiff   D. trencher

B.   11. an indirect reference, casual mention
   A. candour   B. allusion   c. interposition   d. exhortation

C.   12. banter, good-humored ridicule
   A. posterity   B. espalier   C. raillery   d. fopperies

A.   13. a predatory bird having a long, forked tail
   A. kite   B. trencher   C. edifice   D. sorrel

C.   14. of extraordinary size or amount
   A. diminutive   B. consummate   C. prodigious   D. insipid

A.   15. deserving shame or disgrace
   A. ignominious   B. disapprobation   C. insatiable   D. erudition

B.   16. read, scrutinized
   A. debauched   B. perused   C. vindicated   D. accoutred

D.   17. fashion at a particular time; current use
   A. comeliness   B. rudiments   C. parity   D. vogue

C.   18. one who lives withdrawn from the world
   A. copse   B. auditor   C. recluse   D. mastiff

A.   19. without dignity or aspirations
   A. grovelling   B. recompensed   C. expedient   D. scrofulous

D.   20. hateful or detestable; obnoxious
   A. vernal   B. inviolable   C. scrupulous   D. odious

VOCABULARY REVIEW GAME *Gulliver's Travels*

OSEDAHH	HOGSHEAD	a large cask
ATQDUNA	QUADRANT	a square; a navigation instrument
MASNEIIOTSI	ANIMOSITIES	bitter hostilities, hatred
YARATIC	ALACRITY	briskness, cheerful readiness
BINLESTIA	INSATIABLE	not able to be satisfied
MENSRICUPTCICO	CIRCUMSPECTION	caution, heedfulness
EEETINDPX	EXPEDIENT	conducive to a result
ZIMNEZ	MIZZEN	the sail near the stern of a three masted vessel
PEPSOFIRE	FOPPERIES	manners, etc. of a foolish person
TABALIA	BATTALIA	an army in battle array or on the march
TEDIRONIU	ERUDITION	learning, scholarship, knowledge
YTIRETSOP	POSTERITY	descendants; succeeding generations
TENHIZ	ZENITH	the highest point; the culmination
RANLIDU	DIURNAL	pertaining to day
TADAMNA	ADAMANT	an impenetrably hard substance
RCANCEYMON	NECROMANCY	magic, conjuration
SUROSLCUOU	SCROFULOUS	swelling of lymphatic glands
NAEDECC	CADENCE	beat of any rhythmical movement
VACOREPITOV	PROVOCATIVE	a stimulant
ROSELR	SORREL	a horse of a reddish-brown color
TRAIPY	PARITY	equality
NERVLA	VERNAL	having to do with spring
NPSGCOTOS	PROGNOSTICS	forecasting what is to come
DIEVTINADC	VINDICATED	set free, defended, avenged
PTIDEMU	IMPUTED	attributed to
MSOSCELENI	COMELINESS	pleasing appearance
SCOPE	COPSE	a wood or thicket of small trees and bushes
SELUCER	RECLUSE	one who lives withdrawn from the world
LOVILABENI	INVALUABLE	treated as if sacred
EOVUG	VOGUE	fashion at a particular time
UDROITA	AUDITOR	one authorized to audit accounts
FADYENEOCRC	CONFEDERACY	a league or alliance
POTHARYGHOR	ORTHOGRAPHY	dealing with letters and spelling
HEADUBED	DEBAUCHED	to cause to forsake allegiance
NIRMEDSAD	PANDERISM	catering to the baser passions of others

MUSNTACOME	CONSUMMATE	complete or perfect; of the highest quality
CELETHARYLIM	HERMETICALLY	closed so as to be air tight
DRETAKCHAPS	PACKTHREADS	a strong thread or twine for tying packages
LIANOSLU	ALLUSION	an indirect reference
FAMTFIS	MASTIFF	a large dog of ancient breed